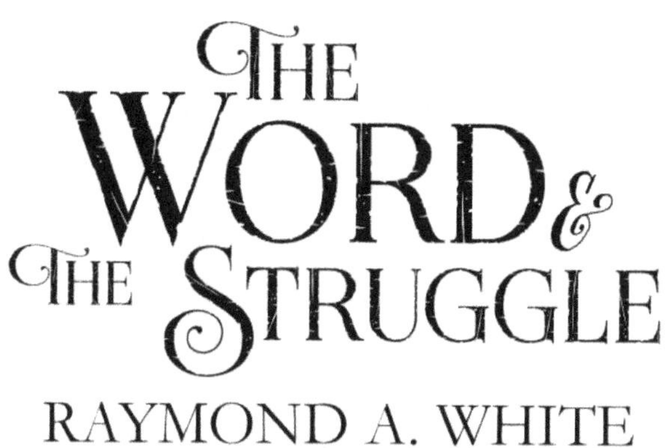

RAYMOND A. WHITE

VOLUME IV: JESUS CHRIST

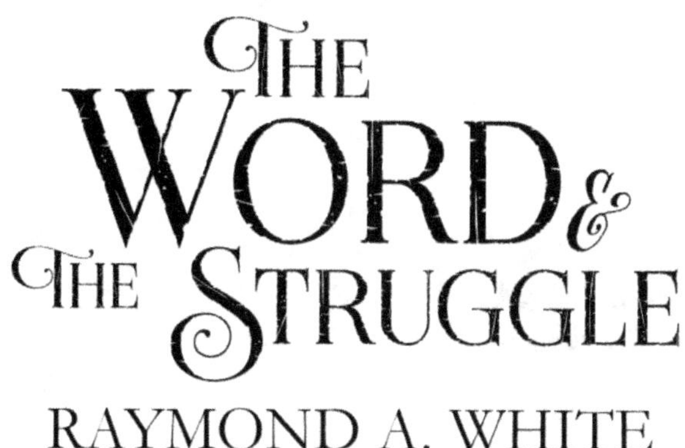

The Word & The Struggle

RAYMOND A. WHITE

VOLUME IV: JESUS CHRIST

SKYROCKET PRESS
Santa Clarita, CA

Skyrocket Press
28020 Newbird Drive
Santa Clarita, CA 91350
www.SkyrocketPress.com

Cover design by Emma Michaels & Rebeccacovers
Interior design by Laurisa Reyes

ISBN: 978-1-947394-16-2

Note: Unless otherwise noted, all scriptural references herein are from The King James Version of the Bible (KJV).

The Word & the Struggle Series

Volume I: The Old Testament
Volume II: The Nature of God
Volume III: The Character of Man
Volume IV: Jesus Christ
Volume V: Marriage & Parenthood (forthcoming)
Volume VI: The New Testament (forthcoming)

More Titles from Skyrocket Press

To Climb a Distant Mountain: A Daughter's Tribute to her Diabetic Mother – *by Laurisa White Reyes*

A Sacred Duty: How A Whistleblower Took on the VA and Won – *by Paula Pedene*

Teaching Kids to Write Well: Six Secrets Every Grown-Up Should Know – *by Laurisa White Reyes*

Relational Nutrition: The Psychology of Attachment and Eating Behavior – *by Dr. Jessica Schulman*

How to Build Your Author Platform – *by Dorine White*

Table of Contents

Preface

My father, Raymond A. White, began studying the Bible in earnest in the 1970s. He used to ride a bus to work and wanted to use that time wisely, so that's when he would read. He quickly trained himself to read in a moving vehicle without getting motion sick, a talent I later picked up as well.

In 1977, our family moved to a small town nestled in the heart of the Angeles National Forest, about two hours north of Los Angeles, California. For the next two years, Dad and Mom built a 2,400-square-foot log home. Dad also bought an IBM Selectric typewriter and his first home computer. It was on those machines that Dad created the programs for our church's Sunday meetings. And on the back of each program, he'd write a paragraph or two on the Bible. He was a big fan of Pastor John McArthur, the founder of Grace Community Church in Panorama City, and listened to every one of his lectures on cassette tape, which he borrowed from the church's library and meticulously recorded for his own keeping. As he learned more from Pastor McArthur, Dad's love of the Bible grew, and so did his capacity to see things in God's word that most of us never could.

Growing up, the Bible was the most common topic of conversation around our family dinner table. Dad was an avid student of early Christian and Biblical history, ancient history, and philosophy. Though he never pursued a formal education in religion or theology (he earned a B.S. in Mathematics from Cal State Los Angeles), he knew more about any of it than anyone I've ever personally known, even fifty years later.

In the 1980s, Dad continued to write his thoughts on the backs of our church meeting programs, but now in La Cañada. He claims that at some point, I urged him to write essays. So, from the mid-1980s through 2013, Dad wrote hundreds of individual essays on the Bible, eventually compiling them into a spiral-bound notebook. His handwritten notes from those decades fill a massive binder, and his handwriting is so small that he fit three lines of writing on each printed line on a page. One practically needs a microscope to read them.

The main focus of Dad's work was the myriad incongruencies in the Bible, doctrines that are, today, a given in Christianity, yet contradict each other. Many of these contradictions have caused division and conflict among Christians for more than two millennia. His belief was that instead of choosing one side or the other, one must accept the contradictions. This led him to title his essay collection *The Word & the Struggle*, meaning it is all right to wrestle with God's word. Even the early apostles and church fathers struggled with it.

As the years went on, I realized how important it would be to preserve my father's writing for his grandchildren, great-grandchildren, and future generations. Many of his theories are, in a word, brilliant. And he has been prolific, a modern-day St. Augustine. Fortunately, about the same time he stopped writing to care for my mother, whose health was declining, I founded my own publishing company, Skyrocket Press. In addition to becoming Dad's editor, I also designed and formatted his essays and found a good cover designer. I organized his essays into broader topics and planned to release at least six volumes. The first volume, *The Word & the Struggle: The Old Testament*, was published in 2018. Since then, it has been followed by two additional volumes, *The Nature of God* and *The Character of Man*. The remaining volumes will be released in 2027.

In 2025, my dad was diagnosed with Parkinson's Disease and dementia, and I became his full-time caregiver. He can no longer make even the simplest of revisions, so that task has fallen to me for this and all future volumes. While his mind is fading, the one thing that revives him and brings a light to his eyes is talking about the Bible. Ask him anything, and many of his old thoughts and ideas come back to him. His favorite topic of all: Jesus Christ.

My father, first and foremost, is and has always been a true follower of Jesus Christ. He served a full-time mission to Ireland in the 1960s, taught Gospel Doctrine (Sunday School) in every ward (church congregation) he's ever lived in, and loves his Savior so much that he still weeps when he sings the Sacrament hymns (hymns about Christ's atoning sacrifice). He raised my brothers and me to love the Lord and to keep God's commandments. My mother, too, was a devout Christian and Latter-day Saint, and my parents both lived exemplary lives of service to God and to their fellowman.

It is an honor and a privilege to share my father's words with you. I hope you will learn something new from these essays and, through them, come a little closer to Jesus. Nothing would please Dad more.

~Laurisa White Reyes
March 16, 2026

Atonement: What Does It Mean?

Romans 5:11

To the Christian mind, *atonement* is the sacrificial saving act of Jesus Christ. Mormons use the word so frequently, and only in that context, that we see it as *the* title of that act, as if there are no others. When most Christians are asked, "In a single word, what did Jesus do for you?" their reflexive answer is usually "saved," which is understandable, since the word *atonement* appears only once in the King James Version of the New Testament (Romans 5:11), while on the other hand, it appears fifty-five times in the Book of Mormon.

Because of the importance of that word to us, we ought to (and do) try to understand it as well as we possibly can. And so, to that aim, here is my offering on the word *atonement.*

[1] The English Word Atonement

The word *atonement* is entirely English and has no roots in either Hebrew or Greek. It was not created by William Tyndale, as some believe, but first appeared about a decade before Tyndale began his translation, just in time for him to make good use of it. The word was not used by Wycliffe.

The word at-tone-ment is a concatenation of "at" and "one" and "with", as Sunday school teachers frequently point out, and they are correct. The idea is to bring together, to unify.

The natural question is this: Does the word *atonement* properly translate the intended biblical meaning? And the answer (my answer anyway) is yes, if we are not too disturbed by some inconsistencies.

[2] New Testament Atonement: To Reconcile

As previously stated, the word *atonement* occurs only once in our English King James New Testament but not at all in almost all other translations. Tyndale (and the KJV) used *atonement* to translate the Greek word *katellagen* (καταλλαγὴν). That Greek word occurs seven times in five verses in the context of salvation. It is translated as *atonement* only once, while the other six occurrences are translated as *reconcile*, which is the word's proper meaning. (Why Tyndale chose to insert *atonement*, an obscure word that had not previously been used in religious contexts, we will never know.) So, to understand *atonement*, we need to understand *reconcile*. Here are the verses:

Romans 5:10 *For if, when we were enemies, we were reconciled to God by the death of his Son…being reconciled, we shall be saved by his life.*

Romans 5:11 …*by whom we have now received the atonement.*

2 Corinthians 5:18 …*God who hath reconciled us to himself by Jesus Christ and hath given to us the ministry of reconciliation.*

2 Corinthians 5:19 …*God was in Christ, reconciling the world unto himself…*

Colossians 1:21 *And you, that were…enemies…yet now hath he reconciled.*

What, then, does *reconcile* mean? It means two people who were once friends, then became enemies, became friends again. Basically, they've made up and set their grievances aside. Therefore, *atonement* is more than just unifying man to God, it means to bring man and God back into each other's good graces.

To further clarify, the word does occur once in a non-salvation context and expresses the same meaning:

> ***1 Corinthians 7:11*** *But and if she depart, let her remain unmarried, or be reconciled to her husband…*

The point here is that if a husband and wife separate, they really should get back together and reconcile their differences. That is the meaning, as a favorite old Christmas song says, "God and sinners reconciled." Let's set aside our squabbles with God and be friends again.

It's an uncomfortable thought that we are God's enemies, but that is what Christians must come to grips with first before we can deal with reconciliation. If someone says to you, "I forgive you," your defensive reaction might be, "Forgive me? For what?" And that's where Christian thinking begins—at the "For what?"

[3] Enemies

That invites the question: When were God and man ever on friendly terms to begin with, so that they could become enemies?

Here are some possible answers. Take your pick.

For those who do not believe in souls existing before birth, maybe we were innocent at conception but guilty at birth. It seems a ludicrous idea, and I don't believe it. Is it possible that, somehow, being in the womb made us guilty of something? I'm just throwing the possibility out there.

Or maybe these verses about reconciliation refer to the fall of Adam and Eve as if atonement is applied to humanity as a whole, a collective event, and not to humans individually. Many Christians call this Original (or inherited) Sin. In that view, Adam and Eve were friends with God from the creation, but the fall made them, and therefore necessarily all of us, enemies of God. But wouldn't that mean that salvation, too, must be a collective rather than an individual event? Or maybe not. Maybe we are collectively damned but individually saved, like a crowd falling into a river off a broken bridge, and life preservers are tossed to each person individually. But if that's the case, then we are collectively guilty—(Of what exactly, we're not sure, of being human? Is that a crime?)—and if collectively guilty, then individual guilt has no meaning, since what else can we possibly do to ourselves by sinning if we are already guilty just by being born?

Or maybe we were born innocent after all and became guilty through childhood as we learned selfish thinking. But that strains from the tug of two objections. First, we don't like to think of children as guilty of anything. And second, there are these annoying Bible verses:

> ***Psalms 51:5*** *in sin did my mother conceive me*
> ***Isaiah 48:8*** *called a transgressor from the womb*
> ***Romans 3:23*** *all have sinned*

So if guilt is from birth, then how could we grow into it?

Mormons have a different explanation, courtesy of scholar Hugh Nibley. They believe in a pre-existence, that we lived with God before we were born. And in that pre-mortal life, we were indeed on friendly terms with God. Then we came to earth, and that was a good thing, except that we also became enemies of God, and that was a bad thing, and therefore we had to be reconciled. So we are talking about both individual as well as inherited, collective sinful nature (***Ether 3:2***, ***D&C 93:3***, and more). Whether you're inclined to believe in a pre-existence or not, you have to admit that it does give sense to the notion of reconciliation.

It's time to put this New Testament *atonement* into the context of the Old Testament.

[4] Old Testament Atonement: To Cover

New Testament *atonement* is a different thing from Old Testament *atonement.* The word *atonement* appears in the Hebrew Scriptures dozens of times and comes from two different Hebrew words *kafar* and *kippurim.* You've heard of Yom Kippur, certainly. That's the Jewish Day of Atonement, that one day each year when the priest offered one offering for the entire nation.

These two Hebrew words, *kafar* and *kippurim*, mean nearly the same thing: kafar "to cover" and kippurim "to cause to cover." To use a modern idiom, to sweep sins under the rug. However, it's not so trivial as that. "To cover" was a Hebrew idiom for "forgive," as we see in…

> ***Proverbs 16:14*** *The wrath of a king is as messengers of death: but a wise man will pacify it* [appease, yə·ḵap·pə·ren·nāh, יְכַפְּרֶֽנָּה׃].

The point is, Hebrew *atonement* didn't get rid of sin; it covered sin, hid sin. But that was good enough, and that covering was the supreme act of God's love to us, as we should cover other people's sins and forgive.

> ***Proverbs 17:9*** *He that covereth a transgression seeketh love…*

The amazing thing about Hebrew sacrifice is that it actually worked.

> **Numbers 16:47** *And Aaron took as Moses commanded, and ran into the midst of the congregation; and, behold, the plague was begun among the people: and he put on incense, and made an atonement for the people.* **:48** *And he stood between the dead and the living; and the plague was stayed.*

That is awesome power. Death was sweeping through the people, and everyone was dying. The priest, Aaron, ran into the middle of that carnage, made an atoning (reconciling) sacrifice, and the dying stopped right there. That priest and his sacrifice stood between the living and the dead. Now that's impressive. Don't tell me you're not impressed.

But still, those sins were only covered, hidden from God's view by the sacrifice of an animal. Eventually, they had to be gotten rid of entirely, not with the sacrifice of an animal but with the sacrifice of the Son of God, which Paul called *katallagen* (καταλλαγὴν), and William Tyndale called *atonement*—not to hide sins, but to reconcile.

[5] Other New Testament Images

But even *reconcile* doesn't tell the whole story. Friends might reconcile after a trivial dispute about nothing; that doesn't mean they were enemies. Tyndale did not want to entirely lose the Hebrew notion of covering sin, so he picked the word *atonement* to kind of bridge the two ideas. *Atonement* has since been abandoned by almost all other English translations, acquiescing to the word *reconcile*, and maybe that's a loss.

However, the Old Testament idea of *atonement*, the priestly sacrifices that covered sin, does slip into the New Testament, sort of, but with a different word. The Greeks had a word, *ilasmos* or *hilasmos*, meaning satisfaction or appeasement. Our Bibles translate it as *propitiation*, which means reconciliation, atonement, or to regain the good will of someone.

Here are some verses:

Hebrews 2:17 *to make propitiation for the sins of the people.*

Here, Jesus is the priest who makes a sacrificial offering for us. He makes the atonement.

1 John 1:1 *He is the propitiation for our sins.* ***4:10*** *sent his son to be the propitiation.*

Romans 3:25 *God hath set him forth to be a propitiation through faith in his blood.*

Here, Jesus *is* the sacrificial offering. He *is* the atonement. The word is also translated as *mercy seat* as in

Hebrews 9:5 *And over it the cherubims of glory shadowing the mercyseat…*

The mercyseat covered the ark of the covenant, and in the ark was the law. When the judge (God) was on the mercyseat, He dispensed justice. But when the priest performed a sacrifice and splattered the blood on the mercyseat, the judge dispensed mercy.

What changed was that in the New Testament, Christ was the priest *and* the offering.

So the Jewish notion of covering sin by sacrifice is not lost. Only the objects have been changed. The Jewish priest is now Christ. The sacrificed animal is now Christ. So Tyndale was right to use the word *atonement*; he just could have used it, I think, in a better place.

But back to Paul.

Paul does not restrict himself to just that one word, *katellage/reconcile*, to describe what Jesus did for us. He draws from a wide vocabulary of different words to paint a variety of images. Atonement or reconciliation is only one. Here is a list:

Reconciliation/Atonement

Romans 5:10 *...we were reconciled* [atoned] *to God by the death of his Son.*

This speaks of friendship. We were friends, then enemies, and now we are friends again.

Justification

Romans 4:5 *...believeth on him that justifieth the ungodly.*

This speaks of law and the courts. We were charged as criminals, and we were acquitted.

Redemption

Galatians 4:5 *To redeem them that were under the law...*

This speaks of slavery. We were sold under sin, became slaves, and God purchased us and set us free.

Ransom

1 Timothy 2:6 *Who gave himself a ransom for all...*

This speaks of paying off kidnapping. We were stolen by terrorists and held for ransom. God paid the ransom, and we were released.

Adoption

Romans 8:15 *...ye have received the Spirit of adoption, whereby we cry, Abba, Father.*

This speaks of families. We are not servants in the house, nor even guests. We are children, adopted into the most privileged position, and therefore equal heirs with God's one natural born son.

Forgiveness

Colossians 2:13 *...having forgiven you all your trespasses.*

This speaks of banks and finance. We owed a debt we could never pay. But rather than foreclose, this bank, God, just forgave the debt.

These are Paul's different ways to view salvation. That is not to say that only Paul used these words. Jesus did speak of redemption but in a different context, referring to the end of the world and his second coming.

> ***Luke 21:28*** *And when these things begin to come to pass, then look up, and lift up your heads; for your redemption draweth nigh.*

That's not the same thing. Redeemed from eschatological disaster is different than being saved from eternal damnation.

So these cafeteria ideas of salvation really do come from Paul—not Peter, not James, not John, not even Jesus discussed salvation in such ways, only Paul. Peter, of course, preached resurrection and salvation, but never atonement. Whatever Peter thought about atonement (and I'm sure he did), he never said. It was Paul's particular task to describe Jesus' death and resurrection in terms of atonement.

[6] The Far-Reaching Atonement

Why Paul? Maybe because he needed so much forgiveness. He was, after all, the world's chief sinner, and therefore God had to reach further to rescue him than anyone else.

> ***1 Timothy 1:15*** *This is a faithful saying, and worthy of all acceptation, that Christ Jesus came into the world to save sinners; of whom I am chief.* ***:16*** *Howbeit for this cause I obtained mercy, that in me first Jesus Christ might shew forth all longsuffering, for a pattern to them which should hereafter believe on him to life everlasting.*

Some people want to defend Paul: "But he was really a good man, just misguided. He thought he was doing the right thing." What is that supposed to mean? Hitler was misguided and thought he was doing the right thing, but we don't say he was "really a good man, just misguided." If we are to judge men by what they *do*, then Paul was not a good man; he was a genocidal maniac who murdered and tortured innocent people.

Don't defend Paul. He doesn't defend himself; he accuses himself of being the world's worst sinner because he was. He killed God's people (***Acts 22:4*** *unto the death*) and tortured them (***Acts 26:11*** *compelled them*). Paul condemns himself, first, because it's true and, second, because he uses his own guilt to make his point. If you insist that Paul "was really a good man," you undercut Paul's message, you rob Jesus of the credit he deserves for his far-reaching love that saved even Paul, and you will probably draw an argument from Paul at his first opportunity. Paul doesn't need your defense; he has Christ's grace. What Paul does want is for you to teach Christ's forgiving love and use Paul's sins and forgiveness as your example.

Paul and Christ are bookends, Paul on one end, the greatest sinner, and Christ on the other, the greatest forgiver. That's why Christ picked Paul to underscore the message.

Do you think your sins are terrible and unforgivable? Christ saved even Paul. That's the point. Christ's loving reach is long. And that's why Paul is the "pattern," to show the world just how far God's love and Christ's atonement will reach. It reached Paul; it can reach you.

[7] The Lasting Atonement

Another important difference between the Jewish atonement and the Christian atonement is that the Jewish atonement works only until your next sins. Then you had to atone all over again. While the Christian atonement, once done, was forever.

> ***Hebrews 7:27*** *Who needeth not daily, as those high priests, to offer up sacrifice, first for his own sins, and then for the people's: for this he did once, when he offered up himself.*

We get an image of this at the Last Supper when Jesus washed the disciples' feet. Peter resisted, Jesus insisted, Peter conceded ("okay, wash all of me"), and Jesus responded to that—

> ***John 13:10*** *He that is washed needeth not save to wash his feet, but is clean every whit: and ye are clean, but not all* [meaning Judas].

What Jesus was talking about is continuance. We don't have to be bathed twice, or baptized twice, or come to Christ twice, or atoned for twice. Once done, it's done. But we do need the dirt knocked off our feet now and then, as in going to the Last Supper, to church, to receive communion or sacrament, to get clean again.

We can't walk through the streets of life without picking up some dirt. That's just a fact. And when we do, some foot bathing is in order.

But Christian security, as the Evangelicals call it, lies in the permanence of Christ's atonement and its eternal hold on us. This is, of course, a whole other subject. But just a couple of verses to leave you with the thought:

> ***John 5:24*** *He that heareth my word, and believeth on him that sent me, hath everlasting life, and shall not come into condemnation; but is passed from death unto life.*

> ***Romans 8:1*** *There is therefore now no condemnation to them which are in Christ Jesus…*

> ***1 Peter 1:5*** *…[believers] are kept by the power of God through faith unto salvation…*

Finally, for my Mormon friends who fret: But once we're baptized and forgiven, we should never sin again. You know King Benjamin's claim that we should have *no more disposition to do evil (Mosiah 5:2)*, that sort of thing.

Well, how's that working out for you? Have you lived a sinless life so far? Haven't, have you? You're just like Peter, have to get the dirt knocked off your feet now and then—right? So, what's to be done?

Here's the point: If you think you're going to live sinless from now on, then maybe you are sinning just by thinking that, because you are trusting yourself rather than trusting God. I'll make that point with a few verses from the Book of Mormon:

Mosiah 4:11 *...even so...always retain in remembrance...your own nothingness...you, unworthy creatures...* [But aren't we supposed to make ourselves worthy?]

Alma 38:14 *...acknowledge your unworthiness before God at all times.* [Even after you've repented and are baptized? That's what it says.]

3 Nephi 28:29 *...there was a change wrought upon them* [the three Nephites], *insomuch that Satan could have no power over them...* [If the three Nephites, the best of the best, had to be changed to throw off Satan, that means that before that change, they were hounded by Satan just like the rest of us.]

Moroni 4:2 *And after...*[baptism, holy ghost, living right, etc.]*...relying alone upon the merits of Christ who is the author and finisher of their faith.* [Alone means relying on no one else's merits; no, not yours.]

Sounds Evangelical, doesn't it—to trust Christ and not trust yourself? Maybe the Evangelicals are onto something.

Does this sound despairing to you? Doesn't to me. I think it's unburdening. If you expect perfection of yourself and think you are hell-bound because you fail at times, you live a very stressful life because you are trusting the wrong person. It's much better to live in God's grace. Live a right life, certainly, but don't let your failures consume your joy. If not that, then what do you suppose Christ's atonement was all about anyway?

However, atonement is not a license to sin. That, of course, is a whole other subject, but on that I'll offer this one verse anyway:

1 John 2:3 *Hereby we know that we know him if we keep his commandments.* ***:5*** *Hereby know we that we are in him.*

The verb "to keep" means to watch or guard over some precious thing. Commandment keepers, when they stumble, have an advocate with God.

Atonement: Gethsemane versus Calvary

Doctrine and Covenants 19:18

Occasionally (though not often thankfully), a trendy sort of "grass roots" doctrine takes hold and becomes fashionable. And while such notions are not quite "false doctrine," they might at least be categorized (in my view) as "skewed understanding" or "exaggerated interpretation."

Most of such notions come and go quickly, annihilating themselves almost on arrival. But one "skewed understanding" (I'm trying to be gracious about this) has gained legs and persists, and I think it's time I gave my opposing opinion simply because I want to. And if you conclude that mine is the false doctrine, then so be it. Everyone has the right to an opinion and to express that opinion, so says the First Amendment of the Constitution, which Mormons believe is inspired.

From my conversations with many of my fellow Latter-day Saints over the years (actually decades), I believe that roughly a third of Mormons believe this particular "skewed understanding" to be true doctrine, about a third reject it, and about a third are unaware that it's an issue and response simply with: "huh?"

The "skewed understanding" that I'm alluding to is probably best called "Gethsemane Atonement" and is understood by its advocates to mean that the atonement of Christ happened not on Calvary's cross but in the Garden of Gethsemane, where Jesus bled from every pore.

Well, I, and many other Mormons simply do not believe that. Further, I and others believe that the notion of Gethsemane Atonement is simply not true and has no scriptural basis whatsoever, and I believe it is time to take this on and offer my opposing point of view.

[1] GETHSEMANE VERSES

And so (sigh) here goes. At great personal risk (I know I'll draw fire), I'll start with the critical verse where the Mormon notion of Gethsemane Atonement is thought to have its roots but doesn't.

> ***Doctrine and Covenants 19:18*** *Which suffering caused myself, even God, the greatest of all, to tremble because of pain, and to bleed at every pore, and to suffer both body and spirit—and would that I might not drink the bitter cup, and shrink—*

The thinking is that if the Lord bled at every pore, surely that must have been a greater suffering than the crucifixion and therefore must have been the true atonement. I'll not quarrel with the first idea, that his Gethsemane suffering was worse than his crucifixion. But the second idea, that his Gethsemane suffering was therefore the real atonement, simply does not follow.

Here's the question: Was this great suffering of Christ in the Garden of Gethsemane in fact the atonement, or even *an* atonement? If it was, you'd think this verse would say so, wouldn't you? It doesn't. Please read the text carefully, and see if you can find the word "atonement" or any of its synonyms—reconcile, justified, redeemed, forgiven—in this verse. Hum. Can't find any such words, can you? That's because they're not there. So why this quantum leap of faith to a "doctrine" that the scriptures simply do not teach? That's a rhetorical question, and I won't offer an answer.

But let's read the text carefully to see what the text *does* say. These words, "would that I might not," jump out as strikingly important. Just what does "would that I might not" mean? The entire clause is future conditional and means, "I don't want to have to go through it." They do not mean, "I don't like what's happening now," but instead mean, "I don't like what's *about* to happen." Well, if Jesus is in the garden bleeding for the sins of the world, what future event could possibly be the subject of His fear? That's a no-brainer. The cross, of course.

There are two other verses of scripture that talk about the Gethsemane event. And it makes sense to ask the question again: Does the word atonement or any of its synonyms appear in *those* verses? Well, let's take a look. Here are the verses:

> ***Mosiah 3:7*** *And lo, he shall suffer temptations, and pain of body, hunger, thirst, and fatigue, even more than man can suffer, except it be unto death; for behold, blood cometh from every pore, so great shall be his anguish for the wickedness and the abominations of his people.*

> ***Luke 22:44*** *And being in an agony he prayed more earnestly: and his sweat was as it were great drops of blood falling down to the ground.*

Neither of these verses speaks of payment for sin, although Mosiah does speak of suffering for sins. But suffering and payment are two entirely different things, as anyone who has ever agonized over an unpaid bill knows. Agonizing over a debt and paying the debt are two entirely different things. "So great shall be his anguish for the wickedness and abominations…" is pain for a debt, not payment for that debt. Suffering grief for a debt does not get the debt paid. *Paying* the debt gets the debt paid. To presume that Jesus paid for our sins in Gethsemane without any scriptural basis, none at all, is to presume a lot. Creating doctrine out of thin air is dangerous stuff, and especially when it touches on this most important of all gospel subjects: the atonement of Jesus Christ.

[2] CALVARY VERSES IN MORMON SCRIPTURES

Now that you see what the scriptures do *not* say, let's consider what the scriptures *do* say. There's a long list:

1 Nephi 11:33 *And I, Nephi, saw that he was lifted up upon the cross and slain for the sins of the world.* Now that's atonement. Is there anything about "slain" and "sins" that is unclear?

2 Nephi 9:5 *…it behooveth the great Creator that he suffereth himself to become subject unto man in the flesh, and die for all men…*

Mosiah 3:11 *For behold, and also his blood atoneth for the sins of those who have fallen…* One might infer that this "blood" is referring to his Gethsemane blood. But that would be a stretch and is clearly not the intent. What is in view is the blood of an executed criminal.

Alma 30:26 *…he shall be slain for the sins of the world—*

Alma 33:22 *…he shall suffer and die to atone for their sins…* Is there anything about "die" and "atone" that is unclear?

Helaman 14:15 *For behold, he surely must die that salvation may come…* How can anyone imagine there was an atonement before the cross? How can that possibly be true when his dying was *the* essential act required for salvation?

3 Nephi 11:14 *…I am the God of Israel, and the God of the whole earth, and have been slain for the sins of the world.*

D&C 18:11 *For, behold, the Lord your Redeemer suffered death in the flesh; wherefore he suffered the pain of all men, that all men might repent and come unto him.*

D&C 35:2 *…crucified for the sins of the world…*
D&C 46:13 *…crucified for the sins of the world.*
D&C 53:2 *…crucified for the sins of the world…*
D&C 54:1 *…crucified for the sins of the world—*

Monotonous, isn't it? How can we believe anything else?
Okay, that pretty much wraps up the Mormon scriptures on this subject.

[3] Calvary Verses in the Bible

Now to the Bible verses. I offered the Mormon verses first lest anyone object to my Bible verses, claiming something like, "Hey! Those are Bible verses. Maybe they're mistranslated." I hate that. There are mistakes in the King James Version, that is true, but not in these critical verses that are the heart of the matter.

Romans 5:10 *For if, when we were enemies, we were reconciled to God by the death of his Son…*

You must understand that "reconciled" and "atoned" are two translations of the same Greek word, *katallage.* They are not merely two words with the same meaning, they are the same word. So, what caused the atonement? The death of his son.

> ***1 Corinthians 1:18*** *For the preaching of the cross is to them that perish foolishness; but unto us who are saved it is the power of God.*

It is impossible to overstate the grandness of this verse. To people who are damned, the cross is foolishness. To people who are saved, it is God's power. I've heard people in church ridicule the cross as merely a torture device. But that's the point. It is the symbol of God's love because that is what Christ was willing to endure for us. It also symbolizes His power because He defeated it.

Actually, there is a mistranslation in this verse, but it's not pertinent to the subject. Still, to be thorough, the offending words here are "are saved" in the present perfect tense. The Greek *sozo* σώζω is present progressive and should be translated "being saved," which is how it appears in many contemporary translations. But don't jump to conclusions. The present perfect tense "are saved" does appear elsewhere in the New Testament. But back to the subject.

> ***2 Corinthians 5:21*** *For he hath made him to be sin for us, who knew no sin…*

[4] Gethsemane: What Happened There?

Now we're getting back to the original question but from a different angle. If the atonement did not happen in Gethsemane, what *did* happen in Gethsemane? Let's read that first Book of Mormon verse again—

Mosiah 3:7 *…for behold, blood cometh from every pore, so great shall be his anguish for the wickedness and the abominations of his people.*

What exactly is he saying? Christ is not suffering here in Gethsemane to pay for our sins, he is suffering the sins themselves! And that's the critical difference. Now, you may argue that suffering "the sins" was a greater pain than suffering the payment for sins, and we'll have no quarrel. Which was the greater pain is not the issue. Here's the issue: In Gethsemane, he took our sins like a man signing for someone else's debt, and He *became* sin. Then at Calvary, He paid for those sins, and that's where He left them, on His cross.

Now we can untangle this challenging verse—

Alma 34:11 *Now there is not any man that can sacrifice his own blood which will atone for the sins of another.*

What? Christ can't pay for *your* sins? Exactly so. They had to first become *His* sins. That's the magnificent point. They were our sins, but He *took* them and made them His own, then He paid for them, which only He could do because he was sinless.

Onward—

Colossians 2:14 *Blotting out the handwriting of ordinances that was against us, which was contrary to us, and took it out of the way, nailing it to his cross.*

Let's go through this verse carefully. What is the "handwriting of ordinances that was against us"? The ordinances is God's law. The handwriting is the written law that we cannot refute. It says what it says. It is "against us" because we broke it and stand condemned. ***Romans 6:23*** *For the wages of sin is death…* But Christ eliminated its condemnation by "nailing it to his cross," as if to say, "Here's the broken law, and here's the payment."

Have you ever nailed a bulletin on a wall for everyone to see? That's the idea here. The law, its demands, our failure, our condemnation, and His payment are hanging on His cross for all the world, and angels, and demons, to see, so that no one can argue against it. A bulletin to the universe: "Paid in full." It's done.

To finally dispel any notion of the atonement happening anywhere other than Calvary's Cross, I have one more verse—

> ***1 Peter 2:24*** *Who his own self bare our sins <u>in his own body</u> on the tree, that we, being dead to sins, should live unto righteousness: by whose stripes ye were healed.*

If our sins were paid for in Gethsemane, then what in the world did he take to the cross if our sins were already taken care of? There'd be nothing left *to* take! Do you get it yet? But He didn't take nothing, He took something, our sins, to His cross, nailed them there, and that's where they remain today and forever.

Every verse that speaks of atonement has this single message: Christ's death on the cross paid for and atoned for our sins. That payment did not occur anywhere else.

So that leaves us with this question: What exactly did happen in Gethsemane? Bruce R. McConkie, I think, said it best in his *Doctrinal New Testament Commentary*, volume 1, page 776: "The saviour took upon himself the burden of the sins of mankind." That, I believe, is exactly what happened. In the garden, He came face to face with all the sins of the human race and somehow transferred them all onto Himself. He "took" the debt and assigned it to Himself. And when He left the garden, they were His to dispose of on the cross. In the garden, He took them, and on the cross, He unloaded them. Taking them was transference, not atonement. Unloading them was atonement.

And what about between the garden and the cross? Well, there is this—

Isaiah 53:5 *…with his stripes we were healed.*

His torture in the garden, his torture on the cross, and all his torture in between, all worked toward our salvation. What a magnificent, infinitely powerful love He had for us. How can we do anything but love Him back?

[5] The Iron Rod

I think there is not much left to say. I've made the case, and what it means to you is now up to you. Perhaps there is one last thing to say, and that is how important it is to let the scriptures speak for themselves without trying to make them say something different than what they actually say. So, with that in mind, I'll leave you with these—

> ***1 Nephi 15:23*** *And they said unto me: what meaneth the rod of iron…?* ***:24*** *And I said unto them that it was the word of God…*

There's a reason the iron rod is not a rubber rod.

2 Peter 3:16 *…which they that are unlearned and unstable wrest* [twist] *as they do also the other scriptures unto their own destruction.*

The Beatitudes

Matthew 5:1-12

> ***Matthew 5:1*** *And seeing the multitudes, he went up into a mountain: and when he was set, his disciples came unto him:* ***:2*** *And he opened his mouth, and taught them, saying…*

The Sermon on the Mount, comprising three chapters in the New Testament, begins with the Beatitudes. There are eight of them, and they are foundational attitudes for life. Some have whimsically called them Be-attitudes, and so they are. They are the keynote for everything else Jesus is about to say in this sermon. And each begins with "Blessed are…" which means "Happy are…"

[1] Poor In Spirit

> ***Matthew 5:3*** *Blessed are the poor in spirit: for theirs is the kingdom of heaven.*

Of the eight Beatitudes, why is this one first? Because no one ever entered the presence of God on the basis of pride. Poverty of spirit is the only way in. You cannot be filled until you are empty. Truth eludes the prideful, so humility must be first.

> ***Proverbs 16:5*** *Everyone that is proud in his heart is an abomination to the Lord.*

This, of course, is the opposite of the world's message, which is, "I'm okay, you're okay." That's comforting, but it's simply not true. God has another message for us, and it's not one that people are generally happy with.

> **Romans 3:9** *We have before proved both Jews and gentiles that they are all under sin.* **:10** *As it is written, There is none righteous, no not one.*

Depressing, isn't it? If God is kind, why does he say this to us? Why not tell us how good we are, make us feel good about ourselves? It's like, suppose you had cancer and your doctor, sensitive to your feelings, told you that you didn't have cancer. He wanted to spare you the grief. Would that be doing you a favor? That would make you happy, but it would also make you dead. Lying to spare your feelings is no favor. Hiding the truth is not kind, it's mean.

But God is kind, so he tells us the truth so we can do something about it. The hard part is believing it. When we realize that we are sinners, that is being "poor in spirit."

Now, just how poor is poor? There are two Greek words for poor: *penes* (πένης) and *ptochos* (ςτωχός). Penes means so poor that one has to work. Ptochos means so poor that one has to beg. And there's a big difference between the working poor and the homeless poor. Which is the word that Jesus uses here in this first Beatitude? Ptochos is the word here: begging poor, without anything, no spirit left, so empty, so without that they have to beg to receive what someone else has earned and gives freely. No wonder Paul wrote:

> **Philippians 3:9** *…not having mine own righteousness but the righteousness of God.*

Does that mean we should be sad? Well, we should mourn (next beatitude), but we should also rejoice because Jesus said, "for theirs is the kingdom of heaven." How wonderful it is to be loved by someone who accepts the unacceptable.

[2] MOURN

> ***Matthew 5:4*** *Blessed are they that mourn: for they shall be comforted.*

Or, in other words, happy are the sad, an oxymoron if ever there was one. What could Jesus possibly have meant by it? One thing is certain: the pleasure-crazed world could never accept such an idea. Nonetheless, it is a familiar experience to Christian believers, this sadness that brings happiness.

There are lots of things to be sad about. Sometimes sadness is appropriate, for instance:

> ***Jeremiah 9:1*** *Oh that my head were waters, and mine eyes a fountain of tears, that I might weep day and night for the slain of the daughters of my people!*

Jeremiah mourned for the women who were raped and killed by their enemies. Who do we mourn? The tens of millions of slaughtered unborn babies? Children who are abused and neglected? The tragic loss of our loved ones? There are many appropriate reasons to mourn, but this verse is specifically aimed at those who mourn for their own sins and shortcomings.

Now, sometimes sadness is inappropriate, as for instance when Ahab got all upset because he couldn't have someone else's vineyard.

1 Kings 21:4 *And Ahab came into his house heavy and displeased because of the word which Naboth the Jezreelite had spoken to him: for he had said, I will not give thee the inheritance of my fathers. And he laid him down upon his bed, and turned away his face and would eat no bread.*

His wife Jezebel gave him some advice: murder Naboth. They did. Ahab got the field.

And then there was Amnon, David's son.

2 Samuel 13:2 *And Amnon was so vexed, that he fell sick for his sister Tamar…*

Amnon was not lovesick, he was lust-sick—for his own sister. His friend Jonadab gave him some advice: rape Tamar. He did. Then he abandoned her.

Clearly, there is a right sadness and a wrong sadness. And just as clearly, Jesus never meant that God would comfort those who use sadness as an excuse to sin, like, "Oh, I'm so deprived, I want what I want, so I'll go ahead and steal what I need," or "kill my own baby," or whatever.

When Jesus said, "Blessed are they that mourn," he meant those who mourn over what made them poor in spirit; that is, sin. God comforts those whose mourning leads them away from sin, not those whose mourning leads them to sin. It is right to feel sad about things that are wrong. Sin, ours and others', should cause mourning.

Isaiah 6:5 *Woe is me…because I am a man of unclean lips and I dwell in the midst of a people of unclean lips.*

2 Corinthians 7:10 *Godly sorrow worketh repentance to salvation.*

People who say you should never feel sorrow are wrong. Sorrow has purpose. Guilt has purpose. Those who never feel sorrow for sin never feel God's comfort. Ironically, they are ill-prepared for grief and vulnerable to being destroyed by it. But those who mourn for sin have a shield against grief: faith. So God comforts us, in this life and in the next.

Revelation 21:4 *God shall wipe away all tears from their eyes; and there shall be no more death, neither sorrow, nor crying…*

[3] Meek

Matthew 5:5 *Blessed are the meek: for they shall inherit the earth.*

Jesus was not what the Jews had expected. They had expected a deliverer as spoken of in ***Daniel 7:14*** *And there was given him dominion, and glory, and a kingdom…* That's what Herod thought (***Matthew 2:3***), and John the Baptist (***Matthew 11:3***), and the hosanna shouting multitude (***Matthew 21:9***), and what Jesus' own disciples thought (***Acts1:6***).

But Jesus had a different message. Rather than conquest, he taught meekness. The world, he said, will not belong to the violent but to the meek, the gentle. They shall inherit the earth.

What exactly is meekness? Well, first of all, meekness is not weakness. Jesus said, ***Matthew 11:29*** *I am meek and lowly of heart*, and then he cleansed the temple. There was nothing weak about Jesus. Why did he do that, cleanse the temple? Because it needed cleansing. It would be too simple if meekness meant cowardice. It does not. Meekness is often a characteristic of great people, mild by nature but strong when evil needs to be confronted.

Numbers 12:3 *Moses was very meek, above all the men which were upon the face of the earth.*

Well, if meekness is not weakness, then what is it? It is self-control, restraint, and gentleness. It is strength under control. Jesus said, ***Matthew 5:25*** *Agree with thine adversary quickly*. And ***Matthew 10:16*** *Be harmless as doves.* This is the spiritual high ground, but it is also immensely practical, the simple secret for a happy—and prosperous—life. A short temper and a bad attitude never brought good things to anyone.

Proverbs 25:28 *He that hath no rule over his own spirit is like a city that is broken down, and without walls.*

Proverbs 16:32 *He that is slow to anger is better than the mighty; and he that ruleth his spirit than he that taketh a city.*

What do meek people get? Blessings, happiness, and the earth, a place where meek lions and lambs and people once lived together in a paradisiacal peace—and will again one day.

[4] Hunger and Thirst

Matthew 5:6 *Blessed are they which do hunger and thirst after righteousness for they shall be filled.*

People without food get hungry. People without water get thirsty. Our natural impulse is to seek what our bodies crave and do not have. Most people, at least in our country, have enough food and water, so we never desperately crave either. But we are in short supply of righteousness.

Isaiah 64:6 *We are all as an unclean thing, and all our righteousnesses are as filthy rags.*

The shortage of righteousness is enough to make anyone hunger for it. Well, not quite anyone. There are people who starve to death and don't know it. That is called anorexia nervosa, an aversion to food. That's what the world has: a spiritual anorexia, no righteousness and no hunger for it.

If we go too long without food, we die, whether we crave it or not. If we go too long without righteousness, we die, whether we crave it or not. In either case, it is the hunger that drives us to what we need and saves us—like the prodigal son whose hunger first made him eat with pigs, then to get back to the safety of his father's house. That's where God wants us, to be safely home with him. Hunger and thirst are good. They drive us to the food and the water.

How can a person in this world not be hungry for righteousness? Children are gunned down, sexual perversion is praised, babies die before they are born, wars rage in foreign lands and in our cities, and our solutions, like gun control, very often only make matters worse. Please, dear Lord—

Matthew 6:16 *Deliver us from evil.*

And there are personal evils that are just as bad and worse.

Romans 7:24 *O wretched man that I am! Who shall deliver me from the body of this death?*

Everyone wants good things. The problem is people want bad things with their good things. People want to be rich, but they squander their money on stupid stuff. Sorry, you can't have both.

People want to be thin, but they can't stop eating the pastries, etc. Sorry, you can't have both. People want true love, but they want sexual sin at the same time. Sorry, you can't have both. You must choose.

Hungry people want only one thing: food. Not a car, not a boat, just food. People who hunger for righteousness want only one thing: righteousness. Not sin with their righteousness, just righteousness. Hunger focuses our attention on the one thing we are hungry for and away from everything else. If you focus your attention on that one thing, righteousness, Jesus promises to fill you up with it, to the brim.

[5] Merciful

Matthew 5:7 *Blessed are the merciful: for they shall obtain mercy.*

Strange words from an age of cruelty, when slavery was legal, human sacrifice was common, gladiators fought to the death, and a male Roman citizen could kill his slave, his wife, and his children, all legally. Cruelty was the norm, the natural man doing what came naturally. In the midst of all that, Jesus called the world to a new life, to do what was unnatural, to be merciful rather than cruel.

First of all, you needn't suppose that if you treat people mercifully, the world will love you for it and treat you mercifully right back. Jesus was the most merciful person who ever lived. He healed lepers, cured the blind, and raised the dead, and the world showed its gratitude by nailing him to a cross. The world does not reward the merciful, it rewards celebrities. So forget about the world's reward. Jesus is saying that if you are merciful to others, God will be merciful to you. And God's mercy is what we need more than anything else.

James 2:13 *For we shall have judgment without mercy that showed no mercy: and mercy rejoiceth against judgment.*

What is mercy? Mercy is not pity. The world is full of people who are willing to shed a tear for someone else's grief. We'll even cry at a good movie for a person who doesn't exist, even an animal that doesn't exist. Remember *King Kong*? Did you cry when he died at the end? He was just an image on a screen. It's easy to tug at the heartstrings. It's much harder to tug at the purse strings. Mercy is not what you feel, it's what you do—not feeling another's need, but meeting it.

Psalms 37:21 *The righteous showeth mercy and giveth.*

There are different forms of mercy. Sometimes mercy costs nothing, sometimes it costs plenty. Sometimes we show mercy to good people, and sometimes we show mercy to bad people who don't deserve it, and sometimes to people who have injured and betrayed us. That kind of mercy we call forgiveness. It's tempting to say, "I forgive you, but I can't take you back." Forgiving but not forgetting isn't real forgiveness. Does God say, "I forgive you, but I can't let you in"? Always keep in mind that it is God's mercy and forgiveness that we rely on for absolutely everything. We should be more generous with it.

[6] Pure In Heart

Matthew 5:8 *Blessed are the pure in heart: for they shall see God.*

If ever there was a longing in the human heart, it is this: to see God, to confront face-to-face the majestic origin of all things, to see with our eyes the purpose of being, to see it all, the fountain of existence, God.

> ***1 Corinthians 13:12*** *For now we see through a glass, darkly; but then face to face: now I know in part; but then shall I know even as I am known.*

To know God as God knows me, omniscience, that is a great promise. But it is only for the pure in heart. Sin has been the gulf between man and God ever since Adam and Eve first violated God's will. How can we cross that gulf? Jesus was asked twice how to inherit eternal life (Luke 10:25, Luke 18:18). He said to the lawyer, love God and love your neighbor. He said to the ruler, keep the commandments and follow me. It is not enough to keep the commandments; one must also obey and follow Jesus.

> ***1 John 1:7*** *The blood of Jesus Christ his son cleanseth us from all sin.*

Jesus bridged the gulf of sin. But is following him enough? After all, there are followers who stop following (***John 6:66***). Where is the momentum to endure to the end? The issue is not just following or obeying or doing any external deed; the issue is the heart that motivates those deeds. Without the internal commitment, the external deeds cannot be sustained. A wrong heart will eventually produce a wrong life, and a right life can only come from a right heart.

> ***Proverbs 4:23*** *Keep thy heart with all diligence; for out of it are the issues of the heart.*

> ***Matthew 15:18*** *Those things which proceed out of the mouth come forth from the heart.*

Jesus said we must be pure in heart. Pure means undiluted, seeking righteousness and not seeking unrighteousness. God wants our hearts to be like pure gold: refined, unmixed, without impurities. With such a heart, one will automatically live a godly life and, in the end, will see God.

[7] PEACEMAKERS

Matthew 5:9 *Blessed are the peacemakers: for they shall be called the children of God.*

When God created the world and put people in a garden, there was peace. When God reclaims the world and restores paradise, there will be peace again (***Revelation 2:7***). God wants peace (***1 Corinthians 14:33***). Jesus wants peace (***John 20:21***). Man wants peace (***Acts 12:20***). If everyone wants peace, why is it so hard to find?

In 1945, the United Nations adopted this motto: "To have succeeding generations free from the scourge of war." There hasn't been a day of peace since then. Humanity just can't get along with itself. Why?

James 4:1 *From whence come wars and fighting among you? Come they not hence, even of your lusts that war in your members?*

The reason men cannot have peace with other men is that men have no peace within themselves. Mankind is looking for the wrong thing. It's been said that "Peace is that when everybody stops shooting to reload."

Is peace just not fighting? No. It is more than that. It is resolving the issue the fighting is about. That's peace.

There is an ongoing war between man and God. They both want peace, so what's the problem? Sin is the problem. God wants holiness and peace. Mankind wants unholiness and peace. People want it both ways: to sin and have no consequences. But sin always has consequences and declares war on God. Without righteousness, peace is impossible, and that's what the human race refuses to understand.

James 3:17 *First pure, then peaceable.*
Hebrews 12:14 *Follow peace…and holiness…*

The two are inseparable: peace and holiness. There is no such thing as peace without holiness. Silence in the face of sin is not peace, but only a truce, and a truce is only a pretend peace, a temporary halt in violence while both sides reload.

Peacemakers are active, not passive. God wants peacemakers, people who rebuke sin, demand repentance, plead for holiness, work for peace between men and God, and men and men. People who do that are the true peacemakers, and they are the children of God. Who are the children of God? They are the brothers and sisters of the Son of God, the Prince of Peace, the one who—

Colossians 1:20 *Made peace through the blood of his cross.*

[8] PERSECUTED

Matthew 5:10 *Blessed are they which are persecuted for righteousness' sake: for theirs is the kingdom of heaven.* ***:11*** *Blessed are ye, when men shall revile you, and persecute you, and shall say all manner of evil against you falsely, for my sake.* ***:12*** *Rejoice, and be exceeding glad: for great is your reward in heaven: for so persecuted they the prophets which were before you.*

The irony of peacemaking is that peacemakers seldom enjoy peace. People who arbitrate wars tend to get shot at from both sides, and people who preach righteousness often make enemies rather than friends. The only explanation is—

John 3:19 *Men loved darkness rather than light, because their deeds were evil.*

No one wants their sins exposed. Conscience is a nuisance that most people would rather ignore. But Jesus wants us to be salt and light (***Matthew 5:13-16***), exposing evil and stinging consciences. That draws fire and brings on persecution. Now, persecution is something we'd all like to avoid—Jesus advised us to be wise and harmless (***Matthew 10:16***). But persecution or not, we must always stand for two things:

Matthew 5:10 *…righteousness' sake…* [and]
Matthew 5:11 *…my sake.* [Jesus]

Our duty is twofold: defend righteousness and defend Jesus. Think about this: The world hates Christ, but he is no longer here. So, since he is out of range, who does the world target now? Who does the world now focus its hatred on? Well, if Christ is in you, the world looks at you and sees Christ. That makes you the target.

But that's a wonderful thing. Jesus took the shaft that death aimed at us, and now we have the opportunity to take some of the darts that the world aims at him.

Philippians 1:29 *For unto us it is given in the behalf of Christ not only to believe on him but also to suffer for his sake.*

If that's you, a sufferer for Christ, then rejoice.

Matthew 5:12 *…for great is your reward in heaven…*

[9] ALL TOGETHER

Now let's put this all together, these eight Beatitudes, and see if we can find a flow, an order, connections that give the entire a sensible meaning. Here's a network that I came up with.

POOR →	MOURN →	MEEK →	HUNGER & THIRST →
You are a sinner without righteousness, begging for righteousness.	Learning that you are a sinner makes you mourn.	You are meek because you have no argument, no defense.	You want righteousness as desperately as a hungry man wants food.
↓	↓	↓	↓
MERCIFUL→	PURE →	PEACE →	PERSECUTED →
Beggars need mercy. The way to get mercy is to give mercy.	You mourn over sin and beg for mercy and give mercy, so God purifies you.	The meek, who truly are meek because they are pure, are the real peacemakers.	You hunger for peace and righteousness, so the world hates you. That's proof that you are having an effect.

You Just Can't Please Everyone

Matthew 11:16-19

> ***Matthew 11:16*** *But whereunto shall I liken this generation? It is like unto children sitting in the markets* [Gr: agora, better translated "park" or "playground"] *and calling unto their fellows.* ***:17*** *And saying, We have piped unto you, and ye have not danced; we have mourned unto you and ye have not lamented.*

What's this text about? What does piping and mourning have to do with anything?

In every era, children play. Back then, it was common for children to play wedding or funeral, the happy game or the sad game. When they played the happy game, they pretended to play pipes and have a party. When they played the sad game, they pretended to mourn.

And then, as now, there were sometimes spoilsport children who did not want to play any game at all. They just sat on the sidelines and ridiculed the other children.

The playing children tried to entice the spoil sports: "Come on," they'd say, "and play wedding with us. It's fun."

"Naw," the spoil sports would insist. "That's a dumb game."

So the playing children would change their game. "How about a funeral game then. That's fun too. Now will you play?"

But the spoilsport children persisted: "Naw, that's even dumber than the other game."

And so the spoilsport children never played any game; they just left in a huff.

John the Baptist brought a sad message, a mourning message. He was an ascetic who wore camel's hair. He spent his time in the deserts, and the people had to come to him in dreary places. He wouldn't go to parties, he had no social life, and his message was repent or be cast into fire. His was a sad, frightening message, and many Jews didn't like him much.

Here's what they said about John:

> ***Matthew 11:18*** *He hath a devil.*

John was crazy, they said. Only a crazy man would live like John.

Then Jesus came, and he was different. He went to the people instead of making them come to him. He went to their parties and their weddings and their feasts. Unlike John, Jesus was at the center of Jewish social life. His message was grace, the happy message. He healed people, and he forgave people. And how did people feel about that? Here's what they said about Jesus:

> ***Matthew 11:19*** *Behold a man gluttonous, and a winebibber, a friend of publicans and sinners.*

How very odd. The very things they claimed to dislike about John were not true of Jesus, but they didn't like him any better. They just had to make up a new list of things not to like. They didn't like John because he wouldn't mingle. They didn't like Jesus because he did mingle. You just can't please some people no matter what you do.

Do you want a God of judgment or a God of grace? The fact is, he is both. Some people, though, don't want either. Like spoiled children, they just want to take their ball and go home.

Christmas Magic

Matthew 2

Who were the magi? Where did they come from? How did they know there would even be a Christ, when he'd be born, and where he'd be born? All Matthew tells us is that they saw his star in the East, and that tells us precious little. How did they know that the star meant anything at all? Surely there is a story, a long story, behind this brief episode in Matthew's gospel.

So let's grope back in time and see what we can learn about Magi.

[1] Medes

Our Christmas cards frequently show three magi, riding on camels, and dressed in Arab garb. None of that comes from Matthew. There were not three, not Casper, Belteshazzar, or Micleor, whose skulls were supposedly found in the twelfth century by the Bishop of Cologne. No one knows if they rode camels; maybe they rode horses. And they weren't Arabs from Arabia, they were most likely Persians from Persia.

Herodotus wrote that the Magi were a priestly tribe of the Medes. They were monotheistic, they used altars for sacrifice, and had a perpetual flame. Their sacrificed animals were eaten by both the offerers and the priests, and they also distinguished between clean and unclean animals. They were, therefore, a Magian Priesthood, similar in many respects to the Levitical priests of Israel.

But the Magi were more than just religious leaders. They were highly influential in government matters as well. During Jesus' lifetime, Strabo wrote that the Magi formed the upper house of the Megistane council, whose duties included electing kings of the Parthian empire (Strabo, XI, ix, 3)—similar, I suppose, to the American Senate, which approves Supreme Court Justices. That would make them, quite literally, Persian king makers.

The biblical connection begins with the Greek word *Magoi* in Matthew 2. Some versions (KJV) translate the word as *wise men* while others (NIV) transliterate it to *magi*. Earlier, in the 3rd century BCE, the Greek Septuagint translated a Hebrew word in Daniel 2:2 to the Greek word *Magos*, which the King James renders as magicians who were astrologers and sorcerers.

So, putting this all together, we get an interesting picture of who the Magi were. They were a priestly tribe of the Medes, astrologers and sorcerers, who were also in the Babylonian court, and who, later, during the life of Jesus, were high in the Parthian government and elected kings. That's the back story.

By the way, the Medes still exist today. They are the Kurds. You know, that tough bunch in northern Iraq and southern Turkey.

[2] JEREMIAH

So now let's track these magi back to as far as we can to see how they might have been influenced by Jewish prophets.

Let's recall that the ten northern tribes of Israel were conquered by Assyria. Then, the southern tribe of Judah was conquered by the Babylonians. Then the Babylonians were conquered by the Persians and the Medes. Then later, the Persians and the Medes were conquered by the Greeks. And still later, the Greeks were conquered by the Romans. Well, the Greeks were not really conquered by the Romans; they just sort of acquiesced to them. But whatever.

The first appearance of magi in the Bible was long before the Persian conquest. When Nebuchadnezzar and his Babylonian army marched into Jerusalem, his entourage included a man named Nergalsharezer Rabmag.

> ***Jeremiah 39:3*** *And all the princes of the king of Babylon came in, and sat in the middle gate, even Nergalsharezer, Samgarnebo, Sarsechim, Rabsaris, Nergalsharezer, Rabmag, with all the residue of the princes of the king of Babylon.*

This word Rabmag was not a name but a title, and it means "head of the magicians," or "head of the magi." Later on, the Magi and the Medes were allied with the Persians, but at this earlier time, they appear to be associated with the Babylonians.

> ***Jeremiah 39:11*** *Now Nebuchadnezzar king of Babylon gave charge concerning Jeremiah to Nebuzaradan the captain of the guard, saying,* ***:12*** *Take him, and look well to him, and do him no harm; but do unto him even as he shall say unto thee.* ***:13*** *So Nebuzaradan the captain of the guard sent Nebushasban, Rabsaris, and Nergalsharezer, Rabmag, and all the king of Babylon's princes;* ***:14*** *Even they sent, and took Jeremiah out of the court of the prison, and committed him unto Gedeliah, the son of Ahikam the son of Shaphan, that he should carry him home: so he dwelt among the people.*

What we learn here is that when Nebuchadnezzar entered Jerusalem, he knew who his friends were, and he considered Jeremiah a friend. And Jeremiah was Babylon's friend—Jeremiah had tried to persuade Zedekiah, king of Judah, not to rebel against Babylon (advice he ignored). And so Nebuchadnezzar's first order of business was to deliver Jeremiah from prison and escort him safely home. Among the princes who were tasked to do that was Nergalsharezer, Rabmag. And so what we have here, apparently, is the first documented contact between a Magi and a Jewish prophet, and it was on the most friendly of terms imaginable.

Later, however, God did not look favorably on Babylon, and Jeremiah prophesied against it.

> ***Jeremiah 51:57*** *And I will make drunk her princes, and her wise men…*

This label "wise men" may or may not be a reference to magi in Babylon's government. But be patient, you are about meet Nebuchadnezzar's magi.

So far, what we have learned is that there were magi, one anyway, in Nebuchadnezzar's entourage as the Babylonians entered Jerusalem. Let's find some others.

[3] DANIEL IN BABYLON

Before Jerusalem fell to Babylon's military might, there were already Jews in Babylon. They were young men, not prisoners, but more like exchange students taken to Babylon to create a cross-cultural experience. Among this group was a boy prophet named Daniel and his three friends: Hananiah, Mishael, and Azariah.

Here's the story in a nutshell. King Nebuchadnezzar had a bad dream. He wanted to know what it meant, so he asked his wise men, his magicians, his magi, what it meant. But he suspected they were charlatans, so he tested them by demanding that *they* tell *him* what the dream was. In other words, "If you're so smart, you figure it out." Well, they couldn't figure it out, and so in his rage, the king ordered all the wise men to be killed, and that included Daniel and his friends.

To save himself and all the others, Daniel told the king that he would learn from God—the God of Israel, the true God—what the dream was *and* its interpretation. And that is indeed what happened.

So the happy ending was that the magicians—Magi, according to the Septuagint—were not killed. Daniel had saved all their lives. As a bonus, Daniel was promoted over them all, and they, likely, were grateful and happy to have him in charge.

Here is my abridgment of the text—just to underscore the main characters.

> ***Daniel 2:2*** *Then the king commanded to call the magicians, and the astrologers, and the sorcerers, and the Chaldeans, for to shew the king his dream.* ***:10*** *The Chaldeans answered before the king, and said, There is not a man upon the earth that can shew the king's matter: therefore there is no king, lord, nor ruler, that asked such things at any magician, or astrologer, or Chaldean.* ***:12*** *For this cause the king was angry and very furious, and commanded to destroy all the wise men of Babylon.* ***:14*** *...slay the wise men of Babylon.* ***:18*** *...that Daniel and his fellows should not perish with the rest of the wise men of Babylon* ***:24*** *Therefore Daniel went in unto Arioch, whom the king had ordained to destroy the wise men of Babylon: he went and said thus unto him: Destroy not the wise men of Babylon.* ***:27*** *Daniel answered...cannot the wise men...shew unto the king?* ***:48*** *Then the king made Daniel a great man...and made him ruler over...all the wise men of Babylon.* ***4:7*** *Then came in the magicians ...* ***:8*** *But at the last Daniel came in before me, whose name was Belteshazzar...* ***:9*** *O Belteshazzar, master of the magicians...* ***5:11****...whom the king Nebuchadnezzar...made master of the magicians...*

Daniel had become the top magician, the lead magi. And from then on, whatever he said, they, no doubt, took to heart and took careful notes. (Two apocryphal books confirm Daniel's rise to power. They are: "Bel and the Dragon" and "Suzanne and the Elders.")

Later, Daniel had a further spat with the king. And when that was settled, the king was in further awe of Daniel and his Jewish God.

> ***Daniel 4:37*** *Now I Nebuchadnezzar praise and extol and honour the King of heaven…* ***5:21*** *And he was driven from the sons of men…till he knew that the most high God ruled in the kingdom of men.*

So the king was probably taking notes too.

[4] Daniel in Persia

But that was Babylon. What about Persia?

Daniel was a young man in Babylon, but he was an old man in Persia. Actually, he was an old man in Babylon who had served for many years and then retired. He was brought out of retirement by Babylon's last king, Belshazzar, for a single day.

Belshazzar was having a party when he and others saw a mysterious hand write mysterious words on the wall. The king was troubled and called in the usual wise men to try to read it. They couldn't.

So the queen made a suggestion.

> ***Daniel 5:11*** *There is a man in thy kingdom, in whom is the spirit of the holy gods; and in the days of thy father light and understanding and wisdom…* ***:12*** *Now let Daniel be called, and he will shew the interpretation.*

The king took his wife's advice, brought Daniel in, and Daniel read the strange text. But it was not good news.

> ***Daniel 5:25*** *And this is the writing that was written, MENE, MENE, TEKEL, UPHARSIN.* ***:26*** *This is the interpretation of the thing: MENE; God has numbered thy kingdom and has finished it.* ***:27*** *TEKEL, Thou are weighted in the balances, and art found wanting. PERES, Thy kingdom is divided, and given to the Medes and Persians.* ***:30*** *In that night was Belshezzar the king of the Chaldeans slain.* ***:31*** *And Darius the Median took the kingdom…* ***6:1*** *It pleased Darius to set over the kingdom an hundred and twenty princes, which should be over the whole kingdom.* ***:2*** *And over these three presidents; of whom Daniel was first…* ***:4*** *Then the presidents and princes sought to find occasion against Daniel concerning the kingdom…*

And so a complicated series of events took place. Daniel was brought out of retirement to read the writing on the wall. Daniel read the writing, which said that Babylon would fall that night. Then, just as Daniel said, Babylon was conquered by the Medes and Persians that very night.

Now there is some confusion about who the conqueror was. History says Cyrus the Persian. Daniel says Darius the Mede. It was probably both; the two separate nations confederated together to conquer Babylon, so they probably each had their own king.

In any case, the Medes appreciated talent, and since they did not destroy the city of Babylon (indeed, it became one of the five Persian capitals), and they needed someone in charge, that man was Daniel.

So Daniel, who had been a ruler in Babylon, was now a ruler in Media, the home nation of the Magi.

But, you might ask, didn't they try to kill Daniel? Didn't they persuade the king of Persia to throw Daniel to the lions? No, they did not. The people who tried to kill Daniel were "presidents and princes," governors, political leaders, or "satraps" to use the Persian word, who were jealous of his sudden promotion, not religious leaders who owed their lives to Daniel.

Those political leaders tricked Darius into throwing Daniel to the lions. Daniel survived, and that's a well-known story. And when the lion incident was over, Darius the Median king was as impressed with Daniel's God as the Babylonian king had been.

> ***Daniel 6:26*** *I* [Darius] *make a decree, That in every dominion of my kingdom men tremble and fear before the God of Daniel: for he is the living God, and stedfast forever, and his kingdom that which shall not be destroyed, and his dominion shall be even unto the end.*

The Jewish God, who was worshipped in Babylon, was now also worshiped in Persia. The point is that Daniel and the other Jewish prophets had such influence over Persian religion that what they prophesied would be documented and revered and remembered for generations to come.

So now we need to know, what did Daniel prophesy? And that question brings us to the most important prophecy of the Old Testament.

> **Daniel 9:24** *Seventy weeks are determined upon thy people and upon the holy city, to finish the transgression, and to make an end of sins, and to make reconciliation for iniquity, and to bring in everlasting righteousness, and to seal up the vision and prophecy, and to anoint the most holy.* **:25** *Know therefore and understand, that from the going forth of the commandment to restore and to build Jerusalem unto the Messiah the Prince shall be seven weeks, and threescore and two weeks: the street*

> *shall be built again, and the wall, even in troublous times.* ***:26*** *And after threescore and two weeks, shall Messiah be cut off, but not for himself...*

This is indeed the most important prophecy of the Old Testament. First, because it specifically prophesies of the coming Messiah. But as importantly, it gives a precise calendar that is pegged to a specific event, namely, a command to rebuild the city of Jerusalem.

Here is what the prophecy says: 490 years (that's 70 times 7) after the decree to rebuild Jerusalem will come Messiah the Prince. He will be anointed the most holy and will put an end to sin and will make reconciliation for transgression. But only 476 years into that (62 times 7), he will die (cut off), but not for anything he did, but for everyone else.

This is a very complicated verse, and there are many interpretations, so I won't venture to give you mine. But there are interpretations, some of which claim to pinpoint the day of Messiah's arrival and others to the day that Jesus rode into Jerusalem on a donkey. Whether they are accurate or not, you have to be impressed that 476 years from the time of Daniel drops us pretty much right into the life of Jesus. I know, "pretty much" is vague. But there are better scholars than me, and you should do your own research.

In any case, you *can* understand that this prophecy would have led people in Jesus' time to anticipate a Messiah, and particularly the people of Persia who had had Daniel as their own personal prophet until the day he died.

A side note: All of the Old Testament is written in Hebrew (of course, you would expect that) *except* for six chapters of the book of Daniel. Those chapters, which include chapter 9, were written in Aramaic, that is, the language of Babylon. Why? Because that's where Daniel lived.

[5] Rome and Persia

When Rome finally came to power, the Romans tried their best to conquer everyone. There were three notable failures. First, they conquered England, but they never conquered Scotland; they built Hadrian's Wall. Second, they never conquered Germany. They had troops stationed in Germany for a while, but in a single battle, three Roman legions were wiped out. And third, they never conquered Persia. And that was a particular embarrassment because Alexander the Great and the Greeks *had* conquered Persia. And it wasn't that the Romans didn't try; they just kept losing.

At this time, Persia was ruled by the Parthians, who were one of the regions of Persia. And the Parthians were tough. In 63 BCE, Pompeii invaded Persia. He lost. In 53 BCE, Crassus invaded Persia. He lost. In 36 BCE, Mark Anthony invaded Persia. He lost. And then even a century later, the Romans were still at it. Trajan invaded Persia and fought all the way to the Euphrates Valley. He held his position long enough to Bivouac in Damascus, where he died of old age. Then his successor, Hadrian, looked over the field and, with a cooler head, mumbled something like, "We can't hold this. We're going to get creamed!" So he went hat in hand to the massing Parthians and said, "Sorry about the mix-up. Tell you what. We'll just tiptoe back out of here, and you can have your land back. Okay?" Well, he did. Hadrian got his troops safely out of Persia, and the Parthians got their land back without further fighting.

There was one Roman general, however, who was modestly successful. He wasn't Roman, he was Edumean. And his name was Herod. In 37 BCE, Herod and his Roman army conquered Palestine anyway and held it for Rome, and as a reward, he was appointed king over the land he had conquered. And that is how

Palestine, this middle ground between Europe and Persia, came to be Roman territory.

So, what's the point? The point is that over those centuries, there was a constant tension and mistrust and hatred between Rome and the East.

Now, to add to the mix, here is what some of the historians had to say:

> **Suetonius:** There had spread all over the Orient an old and established belief that it was fated at that time for men coming from Judea to rule the world.
> **Tacitus:** There was a firm persuasion that at that time, the East was to grow powerful and rulers coming from Judea were to acquire a universal empire.
> **Josephus:** About that time the Jews believed that one from their country should become governor of the habitable earth.
> **Josephus:** What chiefly incited the Jews to the wars, was an ambiguous prophecy found in their sacred writings that about that time one from their country should obtain the empire of the world.

Well, now it all begins to make sense, doesn't it?

Then one day, some visitors from the east, magi, king makers, came to Jerusalem. And they asked Herod this question: "Where is he who is *born* king of the Jews?" In other words, "A *true* Jewish king was recently born; we want to know where he is."

[6] MATTHEW

> ***Matthew 2:1*** *Now when Jesus was born in Bethlehem of Judaea in the days of Herod the king, behold, there came wise men* [Magi] *from the*

east to Jerusalem. ***:2*** *Saying, Where is he that is born King of the Jews? For we have seen his star in the east, and are come to worship him.*

"Behold" means "Yikes! Can you believe this?" The arrival of magi in Jerusalem was unexpected and unimagined. Nothing could have enraged Herod more. Herod murderously guarded his throne, as he proved by executing his wife and son, and once again by murdering the Bethlehem babies. Certainly, these Magi knew that of Herod. They were not stupid; Herod's reputation was well known far and wide. After Herod executed his own family, Augustus, the Roman Emperor, was even taken aback and said, "It's better to be Herod's pig than to be Herod's son."

So, why didn't Herod kill the magi? And why were the magi so bold that they felt safe to make such an accusation (because that's what it was) to Herod's face?

The only rational explanation is that Herod didn't kill them because he *couldn't* kill them. And the only way that could be true is if there weren't just three of them, there was a bunch. Notice that Matthew does not give us a headcount, so we're free to use our imagination.

Also notice "from the east." That's not quite correct. The Greek reads, "from the *far* east"; in other words, from Persia, from Iran. These were enemies of Rome, enemies of Herod, and they were looking for a promised divine king of Israel, obviously, to replace Herod.

Matthew 2:2 *…for we have seen his star in the east…*

Magi were in Persia, and Persia was east. That is, Iran. And they, these Parthians, were very much enemies of Rome.

Now, what about the star? The one Old Testament text that talks about a star is—

> ***Numbers 24:17*** *I shall see him, but not now: I shall behold him, but not night: there shall come a star out of Jacob, and a scepter out of Israel…*

But that was not a stretch. The magi knew to expect a Jewish messiah, that he'd be a ruler, and, from ***Daniel 9***, when. They just needed to know that he had arrived, and so the star was their final clue. They were, after all, astrologers—among other things.

> ***Matthew 2:3*** *When Herod the king had heard these things, he was troubled, and all Jerusalem with him.*

Yes, he was troubled. He was angry enough to kill, and that's why Jerusalem was troubled with him. When Herod got angry, people died. They weren't troubled that a messiah might have been born; they were troubled about *Herod* being troubled.

> ***Matthew 2:4*** *And when he had gathered all the chief priests and scribes of the people together, he demanded of them where Christ should be born.* ***:5*** *And they said unto him, In Bethlehem of Judaea: for thus it is written by the prophet.* ***:6*** *And thou Bethlehem, in the land of Juda, art not the least among the princes of Juda: for out of thee shall come a Governor, that shall rule my people Israel.*

There was no dispute about where the messiah would be born. The magi knew what all Jews should have known, but Herod didn't know: that Christ must be born in Bethlehem.

Why Bethlehem? Because Bethlehem is the City of David the King. And since Christ is the Son of David—(***Matthew 1:1, 12:23, 21:9, 22:42, Luke 18:38, Revelation 22:16, 2 Samuel 7:16, 23:5***)—he must come from Bethlehem.

Matthew 2:7 *Then Herod, when he had privily called the wise men, enquired of them diligently what time the star appeared.*

His intentions were murderous. He only wanted to know how long ago they had seen the star, so he would know how many babies to kill. Not even the magi imagined Herod to be so evil.

Matthew 2:8 *And he sent them to Bethlehem, and said, Go and search diligently for the young child; and when ye have found him, bring me word again, that I may come and worship him also.*

It's not clear whether Herod directed them to Bethlehem or they already knew and Herod was just saying, "Go on ahead." But if the magi knew he'd be born at Bethlehem, then why the initial question, "Where is he?" Well, two years is a long time. Just because someone is born in Bethlehem doesn't mean that two years later, he'd still be there. He could have been (and should have been) in Jerusalem, being taken care of by the royal family. So the question "where is he?" makes sense. It must have been a surprise that he was probably still in Bethlehem.

Matthew 2:9 *When they had heard the king, they departed; and, lo, the star, which they saw in the east, went before them, till it came and stood over where the young child was.* **:10** *When they saw the star, they rejoiced with exceeding great joy.*

It's poetic to think they followed the star from the east. But they didn't. They saw his star in the east, prepared their journey, took their journey, and two years later arrived in Jerusalem. And they must have certainly been surprised to see the star again as a homing beacon at the end of their trip.

Matthew 2:11 *And when they were come into the house, they saw the young child with Mary his mother, and fell down, and worshipped him: and when they had opened their treasures, they presented unto him gifts; gold, and frankincense, and myrrh.*

These three gifts were very appropriate for the occasion. Gold is a gift for a king, and that's what they came for, to find and identify a Jewish king. They were, after all, kingmakers. Frankincense was a gift for God, used in the temple. And Myrrh was a gift for, of all things, a corpse. It was used to embalm the dead. Mary must have thought, what a strange gift. Or maybe she knew, and grieved.

But they were all very practical, the more so since they had to flee from Herod's wrath. Those gifts financed Joseph and Mary's trip to Egypt until they could get financially settled there.

God gives us so much; isn't it nice when we can give something back? The magi had just that opportunity.

[7] Epilog

The miraculous birth of Jesus was no incidental thing. Everything happened exactly the way it did because everything *had* to happen exactly the way it did. And Jesus knew it. And his followers knew it.

John 18:37 *…To this end was I born…*

Jesus reflected back to the beginning, to his birth. It was the virgin birth that set him on the course of his destiny.

Peter also understood the significance of the story's beginning.

Acts 4:27 *…thy holy child Jesus…* ***:30*** *…thy holy child Jesus.*

Peter was fixed on Jesus' son-ness. Even as an older man, Peter had not forgotten that Jesus is God's literal son. That fact is central to the entire gospel message.

John, too, understood that the beginning of the story was the driver for the entire story, the whole Christian message.

> ***John 20:31*** *But these things are written, that ye might believe that Jesus is the Christ, the son of God…*

That, then, is the Christmas story. Merry Christmas.

What Did Christmas Mean to Jesus?

Philippians 2:6-7, Luke 2:7-12

I know what Christmas means to me: the dawn of redeeming grace, God and sinners reconciled, peace to men on earth. But what does Christmas mean to him, the Mighty God, the Everlasting Father, who stepped down from his throne on high to become flesh in Mary's womb?

[1] His Motive

For starters, he didn't come because we were seeking him.
Romans 3:11 *There is none that understandeth, there is none that seeketh after God.*

And he didn't come because we loved him.
1 John 4:11 *Herein is love, not that we loved God, but that he loved us and sent his son.*

He came because he sought us.
Luke 19:10 *For the son of man is come to seek and to save that which was lost.*

And because he loved us.
John 3:16 *For God so loved the world that he gave his only begotten Son…*

That's why he came: to find and save us. And why did he do that? Because he loved us.

[2] His Station

How much did he love us? Certainly, we see His infinite love revealed by His infinite sacrifice. But His great love was shown long before then. It was revealed to us on that first Christmas day when the Son of God came to earth. To see that love, we must see just what He gave up to get here. Then we can see what Christmas really meant, not to us, but to Him.

> ***John 1:1*** *…the word was with God and the word was God.* ***:14*** *…the word was made flesh and dwelt among us.*

> ***John 17:5*** *O Father, glorify thou me with thine own self with the glory which I had with thee before the world was.*

These two verses show us who He was and what He had, and therefore what He had to give up. He was with God, He was God, and He had all of God's glory. He had a lot to lose.

There's a story of a billionaire who gave away all of his money and purposely made himself poor, just to be kind. I don't know if that ever really happened, but that would be a very generous thing to do. However, it would be a small thing compared to what Jesus did.

> ***Philippians 2:6*** *Who being in the form of God thought it not robbery to be equal with God.* ***:7*** *But made himself of no reputation and took upon himself the form of a servant and was made in the likeness of men.* ***:8*** *And being found in the fashion as man, he humbled himself, and became obedient unto death, even the death of the cross.*

This verse is badly translated, but it is the crux of the matter. Here is what it really says:

1. *Being in the form of God* means "having God's nature."
2. *Thought it not robbery* [awful translation] means "thought it not worth clutching."
3. *But made himself of no reputation* means "he emptied himself."

Putting it all together, read it this way: Jesus, having God's nature, thought it not worth remaining equal with God. But instead, he emptied himself—he let go of all his divine privilege—and became a servant, a man, and submitted himself to dying on the cross.

This is not an exact translation; it is merely my paraphrase, but it is what the text, as written in its original Greek, means. Let me try one more time: Jesus decided that it was not worth remaining God, but He walked away from that high station and privilege to become just a man in order to save us.

In addition, there are these verses:

Acts 8:33 *In his humiliation judgment was taken…*

2 Corinthians 8:9 *Though he were rich yet for your sakes he became poor that ye…might be rich.*

And, for our Mormon readers, there is this:

2 Nephi 4:26 *In his condescension unto the children of men hath visited men in so much mercy.*

But that's only half the story. Jesus left home, He walked away from His high station and privilege, and arrived somewhere He had never been before.

[3] His Birth

The story of Jesus' birth in Bethlehem is the most beloved story ever told. There is likely no one on the planet, Christian or not, who does not have some knowledge of the Christ child and his virgin mother, the inn, the manger, the shepherds, and the Magi. Yet, despite our familiarity with the story, some details are routinely overlooked.

> **Luke 2:7** *And she brought forth her first born son, and wrapped him in swaddling clothes, and laid him in a manger; because there was no room for them in the inn.*

> **Luke 2:10** *And the angel said unto them* [the shepherds], *Fear not: for, behold, I bring you good tidings of great joy, which shall be to all people.* **:11** *For unto you is born this day in the city of David a Saviour, which is Christ the Lord.* **:12** *And this shall be a sign unto you; Ye shall find the babe wrapped in swaddling clothes, lying in a manger.*

"And this shall be a sign…" That means *unique.* If the swaddling and the manger did not uniquely identify that one specific baby, it wouldn't be a sign. There might be dozens of babies down there in Bethlehem, but there is only *one* baby dressed in swaddling and lying in an animal's feeding trough. You'll have no trouble, shepherds, picking him out of that crowd.

First: Look only in the City of David, Bethlehem, not in any surrounding suburb. After all, he is the *Son of David* (***Matthew 1:1***) born to receive the Davidic Covenant.

Second: The baby you will be looking for is a newborn, born today.

Third: You won't find him in a baby blanket, he's dressed in swaddling.

Fourth: You won't find him in a bassinet, he's in an animal's feeding trough.

Fifth: And you won't find him in a comfortable, warm house because people don't keep feeding troughs in their homes. So you needn't bother knocking on doors.

Sixth: Where you *will* find him is in some kind of animal shelter where animals are kept and fed. But you're shepherds, you know that. And there is only one baby that matches those bizarre circumstances. Now, shepherds, go find him. All of that was the sign.

"Manger" we understand, "city of David" we understand. But what is "swaddling"?

Today, all newbie's are wrapped in "swaddling," or so the hospitals say. But that's a misnomer. Our baby people plagiarized that word from Luke and gave it a general meaning far different than what it meant 2,000 years ago.

Back in those days, traveling was risky at best. And on any long journey, there was the possibility that someone might die. Today, when we travel, we might take a first aid kit, or band aids, or maybe road flares, or in any case, a spare tire. Back then, they carried gauze, just in case (God forbid) that someone might die and they had to wrap the corpse of a loved one.

How did they carry this gauze? They wrapped it around their bodies under their clothes. Convenient enough. And besides, it might be useful for other things.

That gauze was called swaddling, and it came in very handy for Joseph and Mary.

Mary was almost certainly alone when she gave birth to her baby, Jesus. Does the text say that? The text says this: *she* wrapped him in swaddling, and *she* laid him in a manger. Had anyone else been there—a midwife, an innkeeper, a rabbi, a concerned neighbor—any person present would certainly have dressed and tended to the baby and let the young new mother rest.

Where was Joseph? Probably scrambling to find a midwife. But wherever he was, he left something with Mary that was important and useful. The swaddling.

And that is how the shepherds found them—a baby dressed in swaddling clothes and lying in a manger.

But why? Why did God insist on such poor circumstances for His only begotten son? Couldn't the shepherds have found him just as well if he had been born in a warm house, wrapped in a snuggly blue blankie, and lying in a comfortable bassinet? Well, they might have found him, but God's point would not have been made. To save us, Jesus had to descend below us. It's like frying an egg, if you'll pardon my ridiculous parable. When it's time to flip the egg, you have to get the spatula *under* the egg. That is sometimes a challenge. For Jesus to save the human race, he had to wedge himself beneath us—from his birth, through his life, and finally on the cross.

When Jesus came, he came to save, to be poor (the manger), and to die (the swaddling).

All that was the sign. The sign wasn't only for the shepherds so they could find him, it was for everyone, for us, so that *we* could find him. Jesus offered himself to the world as a Christmas wrapped present. He gave so much that we could receive so much.

And that is what Christmas meant to Jesus.

Be Comforted

John 14:1-27

The disciples of Jesus trusted His protecting power, but they were uneasy when He started talking about dying. They expected a kingdom with an all-powerful king. But earlier, at Caesarea, it became clear that Israel had rejected its Christ (***Mark 8:27-28***), and the kingdom would not be at all what they had expected: ***Mark 8:31*** *He began to teach them that the son of man must…be killed.* And He wouldn't leave it alone. Jesus became obsessed with it, dying, and kept talking about it over and over: (***Mark 9:31, Mark 10:33, Mark 10:45, Mark 14:8***).

By the time they arrived at the upper room for the last supper, they were upset and contentious (***Luke 22:24***). One of them was so upset that, rather than hanging around to be a part of a failed kingdom, he decided to grab what money he could and exit. And so Judas snuck away and betrayed Jesus for forty pieces of silver. That's how tense the mood was.

In the midst of all that—quarreling, pettiness, falseness, and impending death—Jesus was filled with compassion and love. Though He was about to die, what was foremost on His mind was His desire to comfort His friends.

> ***John 14:1*** *Let not your hearts be troubled: ye believe in God, believe also in me.*

But why *shouldn't* our hearts be troubled? If we love Him and He's gone, that's troubling, isn't it? Not comforting. When I lose someone I love—whether to death, or incapacitation in a hospital, or even a long journey—I'm troubled. If I love someone, I want that person here with me, not somewhere else. Now Jesus was leaving. Of course, they were troubled. Why should they be comforted? Because:

> ***John 14:2*** *In my father's house are many mansions* [better translation is "many rooms"]. *I go to prepare a place for you.* ***:3*** *I will come again, and receive you to myself, that where I am, there ye may be also.*

That changes the picture considerably. Suppose your best friend said to you, "I'm moving to Australia." That would be upsetting to you, to be permanently so far from your friend. Letters and emails are not satisfactory substitutes for the companionship that you've become accustomed to, and you voice your displeasure. "Why are you leaving me?" you complain.

And your friend replies, "Oh, don't worry. I've inherited a huge house there with hundreds of wonderful rooms. I want you to come and live with me. You'll have rooms all to yourself. Trust me. You'll love it." That changes the matter, doesn't it?

That's the situation here, between Jesus and His disciples at the Last Supper.

But you're not done with your complaining. You grumble some more: "Australia? I don't know Australia. I'll get lost in the outback. I won't be able to find your house."

And your friend reassures you: "No. You don't understand. You don't need a map. When I'm settled in, I will come back for you. I will take you there personally, so you cannot get lost."

> ***John 14:5*** *Thomas saith unto him, Lord we know not wither thou goest; and how can we know the way?* ***:6*** *Jesus saith unto him, I am the way…*

Okay. *Now* we are comforted. Jesus provides the place, He provides the way, and if you are still insecure about this move, He provides the assurance, the guarantees.

> ***John 14:16*** *And I will pray the Father and he shall give you another comforter.*

> ***John 14:26*** *...which is the Holy Ghost, whom the Father will send in my name.*

> ***John 14:27*** *Peace I leave with you, my peace I give unto you: Let not your heart be troubled, neither let it be afraid.*

While your friend is busy in Australia, settling into the new house, your friend knows that you are anxious, waiting for word. So, not wanting to leave you stranded for even that short length of time, your friend sends to you a trusted companion (*really* trusted, perhaps a sibling) to be with you and to assuage your anxiety.

That's Jesus. Not only does He prepare a place for us, not only does He return to take us there personally, but in the meantime, He sends to us His own truest and best friend, the Holy Ghost, to watch over us and assure our hearts that all is well.

When we die, it is Jesus who will greet us, take our hand, and escort us home. Don't worry. You will not get lost.

Divine Detours

Matthew 27:16-25

Question: Why did the crowd come to crucify Jesus?
Answer: They didn't.

On the morning of the Passover, the day of the crucifixion, the crowd gathered to the Hall of Judgment. They did not come to crucify Jesus; indeed, they didn't even know He was there under arrest. The reason they came had nothing at all to do with Jesus.

> ***Mark 15:6*** *Now at that feast he* [Pilate] *released unto them one prisoner, whomsoever they desired.* ***:7*** *And there was on named Barabbas…* ***:8*** *And the multitude crying aloud began to desire him to do as he had ever done.*

Jesus had been arrested secretly in the middle of the night only a few hours earlier. The public could not have known that (unless they had a telephone tree or texted each other, which of course, they didn't.) But there was a prisoner, one prisoner (actually three), who everyone already knew about: Barabbas (and his two friends). The crowd did not come to crucify Jesus, they came to free Barabbas.

> ***Matthew 27:16*** *They had a notable prisoner, Barabbas.* ***:17*** *Whom will ye that I release unto you? Barabbas or Jesus which is called Christ?*

Now the plot thickens. We might ask, why was Pilate willing to take Jesus into custody at all. He knew this was all trumped up and bogus, ***Matthew 27:18*** *For he knew that for envy they had delivered him.* And he had even received a divine warning, ***Matthew 27:19*** *...his wife sent unto him, saying, Have nothing to do with that just man: for I have suffered many things this day in a dream because of him.* So Pilate had every reason to pass on this. So why did he allow himself to get involved? Here's what I think happened.

Pilate saw an opportunity. Barabbas and his two insurrectionist friends were Roman killers. The thought of having to release a Roman killer in the morning had to have really rankled Pilate. He was probably fretting, "What can I do to get all three of them on crosses tomorrow?"

Then, in the early morning, Jesus conveniently fell into his lap. "Well, what have we here?" Pilate thought. "This is made to order. All I have to do is offer Jesus to the crowd tomorrow, and surely they will release Jesus, their Christ, their king, and I'll have Barabbas on a cross where he belongs." But something went wrong. Pilate had not accounted for every possibility.

> ***Matthew 27:20*** *But the chief priests and the elders persuaded the multitude that they should ask for Barabbas and destroy Jesus.*

There's the proof that the crowd did not come to crucify Jesus. Pilate's plan almost worked. When Pilate offered Jesus to the crowd, that caught the crowd by surprise and confused them. "What? Jesus is here? Under arrest?" they asked themselves. And they would have changed their minds and allowed their plans to be detoured except that the mood of the crowd caused the chief priests and elders to panic. When they realized what Pilate was about to pull off, the priests and elders moved into the crowd to dissuade them from changing their minds.

"You're not going to change your mind now, are you? Remember why you came. Free Barabbas, right? That's who you want. The patriot, the zealot. That's why you're here. Forget that Jesus fellow. He's nobody." And it worked.

Matthew 27:21 *They said, Barabbas.*

Despite the new circumstances, the crowd decided to stick with their original plan: to free Barabbas. And Jesus?

Matthew 27:22 *Let him be crucified.*

In order to save the guilty Barabbas, they had to sacrifice the innocent Jesus. That was an act of cold-blooded murder. But then what would you expect from a crowd that would gather to save a killer? These were not ordinary Jews; these were people interested in Barabbas, these were terrorist sympathizers. And in their hands lay the fate of the nation.

Matthew 27:25 *His blood be on us, and on our children.*

And so it was that a small crowd of zealots made a decision that affected everyone, and it was the wrong decision. They rejected the man of peace, the Son of God, and accepted instead the man of war whose name Bar-Abbas means Son of the Father. He was the perfect counterfeit. That decision set in motion the chain of events that led to the destruction of Jerusalem. God gave them a choice: the life-giving Savior, or the life-taking killer. They chose the killer. The innocent died so that the guilty could go free.

Over the next thirty years, Jerusalem moved increasingly toward revolution until finally the Romans responded by destroying it. In 70 A.D, General Titus and his 10th Roman legion attacked and destroyed Jerusalem and crucified over a million Jews. (Perhaps God avenged that ruthless act by erupting Mount Vesuvius in 79 A.D, destroying two Roman cities, Pompeii and Herculaneum. A stretch, I know, but an entertaining thought anyway. From my perspective, the Romans had it coming.)

The point (well, my point anyway) is that there are times when we are bound and determined to do a thing that seems to be the right thing to do—marriage, business, whatever. But then, suddenly, circumstances change, and that change nudges us to reconsider our original objective. At that moment, we should be most circumspect. Maybe we should stay the course, or maybe we should change our plan. The problem is inertia. In that situation, we are most likely to stay the course simply because it's the easier thing to do. And that may result in total disaster.

The crowd that appeared in the Hall of Justice that Passover morning fell into just that trap. A choice was presented to them: stay the course or change the plan. And they made exactly the wrong decision: they stayed the course. Unwilling to rethink their objective, they crucified an innocent man, set free a killer, and plunged their nation into revolution and destruction.

There's a saying: "There is nothing so unstoppable as a great mistake whose time has come." Well, their mistake was a doozy.

Lives are like that. You plan your life, chart your course, and maintain that course come hell or high water. But sometimes God grabs you by the neck and says, "Turn!" The path you choose, then, your path or God's detour, will lead you to your destiny.

Hallmarks of Discipleship

Matthew 10:25-39

Anyone can claim to be a disciple of Christ, but claiming it and being it are two different things. In these verses, Jesus gives us five principles, five characteristics, of a true disciple.

[1] A True Disciple is Like His Lord

Matthew 10:25 *It is enough for the disciple that he be as his master, and the servant as his lord. If they have called the master of the house Beelzebub, how much more shall they call them of his household?*

In other words, if you really are your master's true servant, doing what your master does, you can expect the world to treat you exactly as they treat your master. ***1 John 2:6*** *...walk even as he walked.* ***John 15:18*** *If the world hate you, ye know that it hated me before it hated you.*

[2] A True Disciple is Not Afraid of the World

Matthew 10:26 *Fear them not therefore: for there is nothing covered, that shall not be revealed; and hid, that shall not be known.* (You are vindicated by God.) ***:28*** *And fear not them which kill the body...* ***:31*** *Fear ye not therefore, ye are of more value than many sparrows.*

You are protected by God, you are loved by God, so what's there to be afraid of? Even in the worst situation, imminent death, God is in control of your circumstances.

[3] A TRUE DISCIPLE DOES NOT QUIT

Matthew 10:32 *Whosoever therefore shall confess me before men, him will I confess also before my Father which is in heaven.* ***:33*** *But whosoever shall deny me before men, him will I also deny before my Father which is in heaven.*

What about someone who confesses Christ for a while, then stops? That's the point here. Confess Christ and don't stop confessing Christ.

[4] A TRUE DISCIPLE CHOOSES GOD ABOVE ALL ELSE

Matthew 10:37 *He that loveth father or mother more than me is not worthy of me: and he that loveth son or daughter more than me is not worthy of me.*

Some people have to make tough choices. Recall the story of Lot's family fleeing Sodom. Why did Lot's wife turn back? She turned back not because she missed Sodom but because her married daughters and perhaps grandchildren were dying there. ***Genesis 19:14*** *And Lot went out, and spake unto his sons in law, which married his daughters, and said, Up, get you out of this place; for the Lord will destroy this city, But he seemed as one that mocked unto his sons in law.*

At some point, you have to make a decision and go your own way with God and not look back, and it may be that your entire family has made a different decision. The fact that Lot's wife had a good reason to look back did not save her, and that's a stern message. Hopefully, that separation will never happen to you, but if it does, you have to do what you have to do.

[5] A True Disciple Is Willing To Sacrifice Anything For Jesus Christ

Matthew 10:38 *And he that taketh not his cross, and followeth after me, is not worthy of me.* ***:39*** *He that findeth his life shall lose it: and he that loseth his life for my sake shall find it.*

What did Jesus mean by "take up your cross"? The disciples knew exactly what He meant; He meant to die. Around 6 A.D., Judas of Gamala led a revolt against Rome. He was defeated by the Roman General Varus and was crucified along with 2000 of his followers along the roads of Galilee. It is impossible for the disciples not to have known about it or even possibly have seen it when they were young. They knew exactly what a Roman cross was and what it was for. And Jesus is saying to them, you may have to face that, if not literally, then at least figuratively. To "find your life" means to secure your personal safety by denying Christ under the threat of violence. The point is this: It is better to lose everything—your family, your wealth, your health, your life—than to lose Christ. There is this saying: "He is no fool who trades that which he cannot keep for that which he cannot lose."

What Disciples Should Be, What Jesus Expects

Matthew 28:16-20

Many people who claim to be disciples of Jesus think that He doesn't expect all that much of them. Actually, Jesus expects and demands a great deal of us. Here's a short list.

[1] Be Available

> ***Matthew 28:16*** *Then the eleven disciples went away into Galilee, into a mountain where Jesus had appointed them*

The first thing that Jesus expects of you is to be available, to be willing to go wherever you are needed. Like the familiar church hymn says, "I'll go where you want me to go, dear Lord." And where might that be? Well, He needed them on a mountain top for a conference. They came willingly. He might need you to be at church instead of out boating, at home instead of out with the gang, on a mission, with a sick friend, at your job supporting your family, at your school preparing for your future. Wherever you go, whatever you do, just ask yourself, "Is this where Jesus wants me to be?" And if Jesus needs you to be someplace else, be willing to interrupt what you are doing and go there.

[2] Worship

> ***Matthew 28:17*** *And when they saw him they worshipped him.*

Men do not deserve your worship—not kings, not prophets, not celebrities, not rich people, not employers, not politicians.

Angels do not deserve your worship. John tried to worship an angel and was reprimanded for it: ***Revelation 19:10*** *And I fell at his feet to worship him. And he said unto me, See thou do it not. I am thy fellowservant, and of thy brethren that have the testimony of Jesus: worship God…*

Idols do not deserve your worship. That was one of the core grievances that God had with early Israel, which led them to captivity. Following that captivity, no Jew would ever again bow to an idol. They had other problems, but idolatry was not one of them.

Finally, devils do not deserve your worship. That is the very thing Satan wants: ***Matthew 4:9*** *... fall down and worship me.* Aand that is precisely the thing we should deny him.

Who then should we worship? God: ***Matthew 4:9*** *…Thou shalt worship the Lord thy God, and him only shalt thou serve.* And Jesus: ***Revelation 4:10*** *…worship him who liveth forever and ever.*

[3] Submit

Matthew 28:18 *And Jesus came and spake unto them, saying, All power is given unto me in heaven and in earth.*

Why would you resist that? All power. He controls everything. Wouldn't you want to be on that team rather than on the opposing team?

[4] Obey

Matthew 28:19 *Go ye therefore, and teach all nations, baptizing them in the name of the Father, and of the Son, and of the Holy Ghost.*

This is a disciple's marching orders: go, teach, baptize.

[5] TRUST

Matthew 28:20 *Lo, I am with you alway, even unto the end of the world.*

So, what else do you need? What are you waiting for? He who has all power is with you always, so get on with it. Nothing else is needed. Are you in his service? Then serve. You have everything you need to do whatever He needs you to do.

What Shall I Do with Jesus?

Matthew 27:22

I imagine that everyone, in this country at least, knows who Jesus is, or at least claims to. Some people in believe him, some don't, but no one is ignorant of the Biblical claim that Jesus Christ is the Son of God, the Savior of the world. There's not much mystery there.

The real question is: Once you know that, what do you do about it? Everyone is stuck with making a decision, yes or no. Maybe doesn't count because not to decide is to decide.

Pontius Pilate is the perfect example of a person stuck with a decision that he would rather not have had to make. Jesus was brought before him, and Pilate had to decide what to do with him: crucify him or let him go.

> ***Matthew 27:22*** *Pilate saith unto them, What shall I do then with Jesus which is called Christ?*

This is the question the world faces, and sooner or later, each of us must answer it and stand by that answer. Pilate tried to avoid the fateful choice, and he had good reason to be nervous. Not only would it be nice to do the right thing for conscience sake, but his wife had warned him of a warning dream: ***Matthew 27:19*** *...Have thou nothing to do with that just man: for I have suffered many things this day in a dream because of him.*

Pilate tried to act on that advice. Three times he tried to pass the responsibility onto someone else, but three times that responsibility came right back to him. God kept dragging him back to the issue: "Pilate, *you* decide. Make a decision."

1. **Pilate tried to pass Jesus back to the Jewish leaders.**
John 18:31 *Take ye him, and judge him according to your law,* Pilate said to the Jewish leaders. But they replied, ***:31*** *It is not lawful for us to put any man to death.* In other words, Pilate, we need you to do our dirty work for us.

2. **Pilate tried to pass Jesus off to Herod**
Luke 23:8 *And as soon as he knew that he belonged unto Herod's jurisdiction, he sent him to Herod.* ***:11*** [But] *Herod…sent him again to Pilate.*

3. **Pilate tried to pass Jesus off to the Jewish crowd that had gathered.**
John 18:39 *Will ye therefore that I release unto you the King of the Jews?* ***:40*** *Not this man but Barabbas.*

No matter how Pilate tried to wriggle out of the fateful decision, the decision was his to make. He was stuck, and he knew it. ***John 19:10*** *I have power to crucify thee, and the power to release thee.* Yes, Pilate, and you don't have the courage to do either. Make a decision.

God has set before each of us, as he did Pilate, a single, simple question: "What shall you do then with Jesus?" We cannot avoid deciding, and absolutely everything depends on the choice we make.

Finally, Pilate tried one last ploy.

Matthew 27:24 *When Pilate saw that he could prevail nothing, but that rather a tumult was made, he took water, and washed his hands* *before the multitude, saying, I am innocent of the blood of this just person: see ye to it.*

Pilate reasoned that if he just didn't decide at all, he'd be okay. It didn't occur to him that not to decide is to decide. He thought he had three choices: yes, no, and none of the above. There is *no* none of the above. When he washed his hands, he knew he was sending an innocent man to the cross. He could have stopped it but decided not to. That was his decision.

Self-proclaimed agnostics think they can escape the pitfall of decision by declaring, "I don't know, so I won't decide." But the problem remains: To not decide is to decide. You cannot *not* decide. So, I will ask you again as God did Pilate: What will you do with Jesus? Don't do what Pilate did. He let someone else, the crowd, answer for him.

A final thought:

Hebrews 2:3 *How shall we escape, if we neglect so great a salvation?*

A final, final thought.

"I shall be telling this with a sigh
Somewhere ages and ages hence:
Two roads diverged in a wood, and I
I took the one less traveled by
And that has made all the difference."

From "The Road Not Taken" by Robert Frost

You Are What You Eat

John 6:51-66

John 6:51 *...if any man eat of this bread, he shall live forever; and the bread...is my flesh.*

Jesus miraculously fed 5000, making food from nothing. Then the next morning, the crowd came back for breakfast. Jesus said to them, you shouldn't have come here looking for breakfast; you should have come here looking for me: I am the bread you need to eat.

This is a good metaphor and not at all outlandish, as the crowd made it out to be. We say similar things today: "My bills are eating me alive," and "You are what you eat." The Jews also had such metaphors involving food and eating.

Psalms 14:4 *...workers of iniquity...eat up my people.*

Ecclesiastes 4:5 *The fool foldeth his hands together and eatheth his own flesh.*

In other words, lazy people go broke. That's not hard to understand as long as you don't take "eat his own flesh" literally, which no one did. Obviously, it's hyperbole. The only reason anyone would take such a thing literally, to be intentionally stupid, is to ridicule the speaker in an argument where you want to make your opponent's words appear ridiculous.

That is exactly what the crowd did to Jesus. He used a perfectly fine hyperbole, an exaggeration to make a point, and they deliberately took Him literally to make His words appear ridiculous so they'd have a pretext to walk away. What was really on their minds was, "Well, if you're not going to feed us again, we're outta here."

> ***John 6:52*** *How can this man give us his flesh to eat?*

They literalized His words because they didn't like His demands. They weren't stupid. They knew He didn't mean "eat me" literally. As long as He gave them stuff they wanted, like free food, they were willing to follow Him.

This is just like American voters who vote themselves benefits from the public trust. We vote for the politicians who promise the most goodies, no matter that they bankrupt the economy.

But as soon as Jesus demanded something from them, well, they didn't like that and were gone, and used a very thin pretext to justify their exodus. Here's what He said, and here's how they reacted:

> ***John 6:54*** *Whoso eateth my flesh and drinketh my blood hath eternal life.* ***:56*** *He that eatheth my flesh and drinketh my blood dwelleth in me and I in him.* ***:60*** *This is a hard saying: who can hear it?* ***:66*** *From that time many…walked no more with him.*

Why did Jesus use such a strong metaphor? Because it said exactly what he needed to say and what they needed to hear. Consider this about food: You can study it, smell it, taste it, philosophize about it, paint pictures of it, grind it, chop it, freeze it, but food will never do you a bit of good until you eat it and it becomes you.

Our nature is death—

John 6:53 *Ye have no life in you.*

His nature is life—

John 14:6 *I am the way, the truth, and the life.*

To live, we need to ingest Christ's nature, by some means, into ourselves. The metaphor is figurative, but it is not figurative to say we must become what He is if we are going to have eternal life. So we must take on the properties of His life into our life—in a picture, "eat His flesh and drink His blood."

Why flesh and blood? There are two issues here: **[1]** His flesh. He came in the flesh, He was born, He was/is a real person, human, not a fiction, a fantasy, a legend, or a story fabricated by Hollywood.

1 Timothy 3:16 *God was manifest in the flesh.*

That is literal and not at all figurative.

Then **[2]** His blood. He died for you. Not just died, but executed as a criminal. Nobody receives Christ without his death. He was not just a prophet miracle worker, He was the sacrifice for the world's sins.

Romans 5:10 *We were reconciled to God by the death of his son.*

Do you want eternal life? Then you have to get *His* eternal life because there is no other. And the only way to get His eternal life is to take Him into yourself. You must swallow (His metaphor, not mine) all of who He is. His flesh, His blood, His life, and His death. Then you will be "in Him" and "He in you." And that is how you get eternal life.

John 11:26 *And whosoever liveth and believeth in me shall never die.*
John 14:20 *I am in my Father, and ye in me, and I in you.*
John 15:4 *Abide in me, and I in you.*
John 17:21 *That they all may be one; as thou, Father, art in me, and I in thee, that they also may be one in us.*
1 Corinthians 3:16 *Know ye not that ye are the temple of God, and the Spirit of God dwelleth in you?*

It is almost symbiotic, isn't it? Maybe that's exactly what Jesus expects, a symbiotic relationship between Him and us, and that is quite literal after all.

The Lord's Fishermen

Matthew 4:18-22

Matthew 4:18 *And Jesus, walking by the sea of Galilee, saw two brothers, Simon called Peter, and Andrew his brother, casting a net into the sea: for they were fishers.* ***:19*** *And he saith unto them, Follow me, and I will make you fishers of men.* ***:20*** *And the straightway left their nets, and followed him.* ***:21*** *And going on from thence, he saw other two brethren, James the son of Zebedee, and John his brother, in a ship with Zebedee their father, mending their nets; and he called them.* ***:22*** *And they immediately left the ship and their father, and followed him.*

Jesus had his choice of men. He said (***John 15:16***) *Ye have not chosen me, but I have chosen you.* Well, if he had his choice, why did he choose fishermen? Why did he not instead choose rabbis? Or scribes? Or lawyers? Or politicians?—people with clout, movers who could get things done in a hurry and jumpstart a fledgling movement? When he chose his inner circle of personal friends and confidants, those who would soon bear the responsibility for the success or failure of the new church, what drew the Lord to fishermen? Maybe Jesus was looking for special qualities. Three come to mind.

[1] Fishermen Are Patient

If any virtue typifies fishermen, it is patience. They wait and wait, endlessly it seems, for fish to bite. Without patience, fishermen simply cannot catch fish, nor can they catch souls.

Luke 8:15 *Bring forth fruit with patience.*

[2] Fishermen Are Brave

The Breton Fisherman's Prayer reads, "Oh God thy sea is so great, and my boat is so small," which succinctly describes the hazardous sea and how fishermen feel about it. The Sea of Galilee is noted for its sudden and violent storms, and only the brave venture out onto its deadly waves. The Lord called such men to an even more perilous work, the work of the gospel.

1 Corinthians 16:13 *Quit you like men, be strong!*

[3] Fishermen Are Impartial

Fishermen are not hunters. They don't line up their sights on their target of choice. Hunters pick their quarry. Fishermen don't have that luxury; they take whatever happens into their net.

John 6:37 *Him that cometh to me I will in no way cast out.*

There's a lot to be said for fishermen. Be a fisherman. Fish for souls.

Why Was Jesus Jewish?

Genesis 44:33, Matthew 1:1-3

Why was Jesus Christ a Jew? By that I don't mean why was he not a Greek or a Roman, I mean why was he not a Levite or a Reubenite?

> ***Matthew 1:1*** *The book of the generation of Jesus Christ…* ***:2*** *…and Jacob begat Judas…* ***:3*** *And Judas begat Phares and Zara of Thamar…*

Why was he descended from Judah specifically and not from any of Judah's brothers? After all, Levi was the priestly tribe, Reuben was the firstborn, and Joseph ended up with the double portion, the birthright blessing that Reuben had lost. With so many choices, why did God pick Judah for the lineage of Christ? And it didn't just happen. It was known in the mind of God from the very beginning.

[1] The Promise

> ***Genesis 49:10*** *The scepter shall not depart from Judah, nor a lawgiver from between his feet, until Shiloh come; and unto him shall the gathering of the people be.*

> ***1 Chronicles 5:2*** *For Judah prevailed above his brethren, and of him came the chief ruler: but the birthright was Joseph's.*

To Judah "shall the gathering of the people be." And that's just what happened.

The Davidic dynasty was of Judah. The temple was built in Judah. When the nation split in two, the true worshippers from all the tribes moved south to Judah. When the ten tribes were conquered and exited their homeland, it was Judah that preserved remnants of all the tribes. And when Judah was finally conquered, when they returned, with them returned remnants from all the tribes of Israel. And finally, it was to Judah that Christ was born, offering salvation to the world.

But still, why Judah?

[2] JUDAH

Judah made lots of bad choices in his life. He hated his brother Joseph, tried to kill him, then at the last minute, decided instead to sell him into slavery. He lied to his father and stood by that lie for more than twenty years. Although married, he had a passion for prostitutes. Yet when his own daughter-in-law, Tamar, became pregnant "by whoredom," he ordered her burned.

Such self-righteous hypocrisy is sickening. Judah lived a life of wrong choices.

But there was one day when Judah made absolutely the right choice, the choice that altered his and his family's destiny forever. Here's the story.

Israel's family was suffering because of famine, and so Judah and his brothers traveled to Egypt for food. They didn't know that their brother Joseph had risen to high office and was the second in command, just under Pharaoh.

They met with Joseph, not knowing who he was. In that meeting, Joseph demanded to know if there was another brother.

They confessed that yes, there was, the youngest, Benjamin, who had remained at home with their father Jacob.

Then Joseph demanded to see this youngest brother. If they did not bring him, they would receive no food.

The reason Joseph wanted to see Benjamin was simple: Benjamin was Joseph's only full brother; they were sons of Rachel. All the others were half-brothers, sons of Leah, Bilhah, and Zilpah. Of course, the ten brothers did not know Joseph's true motive.

This was bad news. Not only did they return home empty-handed with no food, but now they had to report this unreasonable demand to their father.

Jacob was understandably reluctant to give up Benjamin. After all, Jacob had loved Rachel best. She had given Jacob two sons, Joseph and Benjamin, and Joseph was dead, or so he thought. So all Jacob had left of his beloved Rachael was her young son Benjamin.

Judah and the other brothers understood their father's reluctance to give up the boy, but they had no choice. Either Benjamin went with them to Egypt, or they would starve.

In order to persuade their father, Judah stepped up to the plate and did an amazing thing.

> ***Genesis 43:9*** *I will be surety for him; of my hand shalt thou require him: if I bring him not unto thee, and set him before thee, then let me bear the blame for ever.*

Judah offered himself as a personal surety for Benjamin. What that actually means, we're about to see, and they were not empty words.

So the brothers returned to Egypt and brought Benjamin with them.

Now the story gets complicated. Here is the short version: Joseph framed Benjamin with an invented theft and threatened to keep Benjamin as his personal slave.

That was Judah's undoing. Panic overwhelmed him, and all thoughts of personal safety fled. He had promised Benjamin's safe return and had made himself a personal surety for his brother. He was on the hook.

But it was not just his promise that hooked him; it was his own personal guilt, his love for his father, and his love for Benjamin. He knew that he was responsible for Joseph's death and for his father's grief, and now he was about to lose Rachel's second son as well. It was not just guilt that motivated him; it was a deep sense of sorrow for his father's pain that was now his own. He had caused his father pain once; he would not allow it to happen again.

What could he do to prevent this horrible thing from happening?

> **Genesis 43:13** *Then they rent their clothes…and returned to the city.* **:14** *And Judah and his brethren came to Joseph's house…and they fell before him on the ground.*

They came back to Joseph begging. They could have left safely and gone home. But their own personal safety was no longer important. They must risk everything for the boy. But what could they do?

Then, in a moment of extreme courage, Judah made good on his promise and did exactly the right thing. He exchanged himself for his brother.

> **Genesis 44:33** *Now therefore, I pray thee, let thy servant abide instead of the lad a bondman to my lord; and let the lad go up with his brethren.*

That was it. That was Judah's moment of greatness. For all his faults, he, and he alone, offered himself in exchange for Benjamin. "Let *me* live the life of a slave and let my brother go free."

How different now was Judah? Once, he had hated a brother enough to kill him. Now he loved a brother enough to die for him. Once, he had scorned his father and was not mindful at all of his pain. Now his father's pain moved him to self-sacrifice. Once, he cared only for his own station, enraged with jealousy. Now he cared only for others, letting go of all concern for his own personal safety. Once, he had sold a brother into slavery. Now he sold himself into slavery to save a brother. Judah had, at that moment, risen to greatness and made himself the forerunner of Christ.

And that was Joseph's undoing.

> ***Genesis 45:1*** *Then Joseph could not refrain himself before all them that stood by him; and he cried, Cause every man to go out from me. And there stood no man with him, while Joseph made himself known unto his brethren.*

And of course, the whole family moved to Egypt, and they lived happily ever after. I love happy endings, don't you?

But there was more to the story.

[3] The Blessing

When it was all explained to their father, Jacob, what had happened and how things stood, Jacob took it all to heart. Then, some time later, just before Jacob died, he gave blessings to his sons. And this is the blessing he gave to Judah—

> ***Genesis 49:8*** *Judah, thou are he whom thy brethren shall praise: thy hand shall be in the neck of thine enemies; thy father's children shall bow down before thee.* ***:9*** *Judah is a lion's whelp: from the prey, my son, thou art gone up: he stooped down, he crouched as a lion, and as an old lion; who shall rouse him up?* ***:10*** *The scepter shall not depart from Judah, nor a lawgiver from between his feet, until Shiloh come; and unto him shall the gathering of the people be.* ***:11*** *Binding his foal unto the vine, and his ass's colt unto the choice vine; he washed his garments in wine, and his clothes in the blood of grapes.*

Judah would rule until Shiloh come. Shiloh means, "he whose right it is to rule." And thus began Israel's notion of a coming Messiah.

Why Judah? Because he was the one who offered himself in exchange for his brother.

That's what I believe. And then, down through the centuries as the destiny of the tribes of Israel played itself out, it was Judah that survived—(and part of Benjamin, Judah once again protecting Benjamin)—and brought the Savior into the world to save the world.

[4] MOMENT OF DESTINY

For many people, greatness is a single moment. For one, it's risking his life to rescue a child from a burning building. For another, it's giving her blood, her kidney, or half her liver to someone who desperately needs it. I once read the story of a prison riot where a mob was about to kill a guard. Then unexpectedly, one prisoner, a lifer, stepped between the guard and the mob and protected him, risking his own life. Here are just a few unlikely heroes from the Bible:

- A Roman soldier faced down an angry crowd to save Paul (***Romans 21:31-40***).
- Rahab, a harlot of Jericho, risked her life to save two Israelite spies (***Joshua 2:3-4***).
- A very flawed Samson sacrificed himself to destroy 3,000 of Israel's enemies (***Judges 16:30***).

Some people live a life of spectacular failure. And then in a moment of destiny, dig down and find the supreme courage to do the right thing and offer themselves for some great cause.

If that's you, maybe no one will know it. But God will. And in that moment of greatness, your courage and determination will change your destiny forever, whether you survive or not.

When we think of Christ, we would do well to reflect on His ancestor, Judah. He is, in many respects, a picture of ourselves and our failures, and our redemption.

Oh, and what about Tamar, Judah's daughter-in-law, whom he wanted to burn? Fortunately, Judah changed his mind about her and said—

Genesis 38:26 *She hath been more righteous than I.*

Saving her was a good thing. Not only because it was the right thing to do, but because by saving her, he saved the family line that produced Jesus Christ.

Judah was a man of many mistakes. But finally, he repented, saw others as better than himself, and offered himself in exchange for someone else. That, in my opinion, is why Christ was a Jew.

Knowing Jesus

John 20:28

Two Christians died and found themselves seated on a white bench in a great white hallway. Were they Baptists or Catholics or Mormons? Take your pick; it doesn't matter. At the end of the hallway, an open door led into a room. Clearly, they were in some heavenly place.

A voice spoke to them from the room. "Will the first gentleman step in here, please?"

The man sitting closest to the door stood, and, facing the door, he said, "Who? Me?"

"Yes," replied the gentle voice from the room. "Please, do come in and have a seat."

The man entered. He saw that the room was entirely white with only two chairs. In one of the chairs sat an angelic being. "I need to interview you, if you don't mind," said the being who beckoned to the empty chair as he spoke, "This will only take a few minutes."

The man sat in the available chair.

The interviewer continued. "Let's see. You are Brother Smith, is that correct?"

"Yes, sir," the man answered. "I am Brother Smith."

"Don't be nervous, Brother Smith. Just tell me what you know about Jesus Christ."

"Well, there's a lot to tell," replied Brother Smith. "I know that he is the Son of God, that he was born on the earth to the Virgin Mary, he was sinless throughout his entire life, the only person who ever lived who was sinless. He healed people, he raised the dead, he did countless other miracles that only the Son of God could do. Then one day, he was arrested and crucified, but that was God's plan so that by his suffering and death, all the rest of us could have our sins forgiven and return to God. That's the atonement. Then he rose from the dead, and that guaranteed that all the rest of us will also rise from the dead. That's the resurrection."

The interviewer pondered the answer for a moment, then said, "That is all true. But tell me, Brother Smith, what do *you know* about Jesus Christ."

Startled, Brother Smith continued. "Well, I know that he created the worlds and all things. Is that the answer you are looking for?"

The interviewer winced, "Not quite. But that certainly is a very fine answer. Will you please step outside and return to the bench? And please invite the other brother to come in? Thank you."

Brother Smith did exactly as he was asked—obedience was always his strongest virtue.

The second man came to the door and entered. He saw that the room was entirely white with only two chairs. In one of the chairs sat an angelic being. When the man saw the being, he immediately fell prostrate to the floor and declared—

John 20:28 *My Lord and my God.*

How well do *you know* Jesus?

Do You Love Jesus?

John 21:15-25

On the surface, this text seems to be a confident affirmation of Peter's love for Jesus. Jesus asks Peter three times, "Do you love me?" And Peter asserts three times, "Yes, of course. You know I do."

But that English translation is entirely wrong, and the Greek gives exactly the opposite message. This dialog is not a message of Peter's self-confidence and devotion, but rather a message of his lost confidence, self-doubt, and restoration.

To understand this text, you need to understand the two Greek words for love: agape (ἀγαπᾷς) and philo (φιλῶ). Agape is divine love and is unconditional. Philo is more like a strong affection and is very conditional. To bring the truth of this text to the surface, I'll translate agape to love and philo to like. That will expose what this text is really saying.

Now, picture Peter. Having so often boasted of his love for Jesus (***Matthew 25:33, John 13:37***), he now stares into the face of his own failure. He denied Jesus three times. His denial is recorded in all four gospels, so there is no doubt what happened.

Now Jesus asks him, "Do you love me?" If you were in Peter's situation, how would you answer? Here's what really happened, how the dialogue unfolded.

> ***John 21:15*** *Simon* [Jesus no longer calls him Peter, the rock], *lovest* [agapas ἀγαπᾷς] *thou me? Yea Lord: thou knowest that I love* [philo φιλῶ] *thee.*

The key to understanding this text is to notice that Peter changed the word from *agapas*, which means a deeply devoted love, to *philo*, which means to be fond of someone or to like them. In other words, Peter is evading Jesus' direct question.

Jesus asks again, "Simon, do you love me?"

Peter answers, "Well, Lord, you know I like you a lot." In other words, I hope that will do because that's all I've got.

> ***John 21:16*** *...Simon...lovest* [agapas] *thou me? He saith unto him, Yea, Lord; thou knowest that I love* [philo] *thee.*

So Jesus persists, and Peter persists.

"But Peter, that's not what I asked. Do you *love* me?"

"Well, you know that I *like* you a lot." Honestly, what else is Peter to say? How can he affirm that he loves Jesus when he had just denied him three times? That's the issue here.

So now what does Jesus do? He comes right down to Peter's level.

> ***John 21:17*** *...Simon...lovest* [phileis] *thou me? Peter was grieved, because he said unto him the third time, Lovest* [pheleis] *thou me? And he said unto him, Lord, thou knowest all things, thou knowest that I love* [pheleis] *thee.*

Jesus is saying, "Okay, Peter, I can play that game too. If 'like' is all you got, do you even 'like' me?"

Then the text says, "Peter was grieved." What grieved Peter? That Jesus asked him three times? No. What grieved him was that when Jesus asked the third time, He changed his question to "Well, do you even like me?" That's what upset Peter. Jesus challenged even Peter's "like."

So, what did Peter do about that? Suddenly, he was challenged. He thought he was on safe ground, "At least I like you," but now Jesus questioned even that: "Do you even like me?"

So Peter came up with something different. If he was unsure whether he loved or even liked Jesus, he had one remaining security: he turned it back on Jesus. "Lord, I don't know. I don't know my own heart. But *you* know my heart because you know everything. *You* know that I like you even when I'm not so sure."

Now, that's a defense that makes sense. What's more important than you knowing that you love God? God knowing that you love God. Life has its ups and downs, twists and turns. Sometimes you're sure you love God, other times you're not sure at all. But one thing is always sure: God knows that you love him, and that's far more reliable.

But Jesus was not done with Peter yet. Peter said, "But *you* know."

So Jesus replied to that, "Yes indeed, I do know, and here's what I know about you, Peter." And Jesus proceeded to tell Peter what was really in Peter's heart.

> ***John 21:18*** *Verily, verily, I say unto thee, When thou wast young, thou girdest thyself, and walkedst whither thou wouldest: but when thou shalt be old, thou shalt stretch forth thy hands, and another shall gird thee, and carry thee whither thou wouldest not.* ***:19*** *This spake he, signifying by what death he should glorify God. And when he had spoken this, he saith unto him, Follow me.*

Here's what Jesus' response means: "Yes, Peter, I know that you love me. And I know that you denied me, but you never will deny me again. The next time your life is on the line for me, you will die for me, on a cross. Peter, you're back on the team. Now, follow me."

That was the best news Peter ever heard. He had indeed denied the Lord, but he never would again. He knew, finally, that he loved Jesus—enough to die for Him. And he knew that Jesus knew it. Now we might understand a little better why Peter later wrote:

> ***1 Peter 4:13*** *Rejoice inasmuch as ye are partakers of Christ's sufferings; that when his glory shall be revealed ye may be glad also with exceeding joy.*

In other words, suffering and even dying for Jesus is a good thing, something to rejoice about. So there really isn't anything to worry about.

> **Hebrews 13:5-6** *...for he hath said, I will never leave thee, nor forsake thee. So that we may boldly say, The Lord is my helper, and I will not fear what man shall do unto me.*

How People React to Jesus

John 7:37-51

The celebration of the Feast of Tabernacles, or harvest, included a last-day ritual. A priest would bring a pitcher of water from the Pool of Siloam to the temple, and as the people sang the Hallel, the priest poured the water at the altar, fulfilling Isaiah's prophecy:

> ***Isaiah 12:3*** *With joy shall he draw water from the wells of salvation.*

Against that backdrop, Jesus taught the people about Himself. His message was simple: You thank God for water, and you pray for water so you can have a plentiful harvest. Well, here I am, the living water that you need to drink.

> ***John 7:37*** *If any man thirst, let him come unto me, and drink.* ***:38*** *He that believeth on me, out of his belly shall flow rivers of living water.*

Living water means running water, river water that flows, not still water from a stagnant, dead lake like the Dead Sea, which has no life to give. Living water is water that gives life because it has life.

There were various reactions among the people to His message:

[1] Some Were Convinced

> ***John 7:40*** *Many of the people therefore when they heard this saying, said, Of a truth this is the Prophet.* ***:41*** *Others said, this is the Christ.*

There are always people who, when they hear the truth, believe it.

[2] Some Were Contrary

John 7:41 *But some said, Shall Christ come out of Galilee?* ***:42*** *Hath not the scripture said, That Christ cometh of the seed of David, and out of the town of Bethlehem, where David was?*

And there are always people who, when they hear the truth, reject it.

[3] Some Were Confused

John 7:45 *Then came the officers to the chief priests and Pharisees; and they said unto them, Why have you not brought him?* ***:46*** *They answered, Never man spake like this.*

But there are also people who, when they hear the truth, are confused, as were these police officers who didn't know what to make of Jesus and didn't even know how to account for their own inaction. They were asked, "Why didn't you bring him here?" They answered, "You had to have been there. Nobody has ever talked like this guy."

[4] Some Were Contemplative

John 7:50 *Nicodemus saith unto them* ***:51*** *Doth our law judge any man before it hear him, and knoweth what he doeth?*

There are always people who want to "think about it." Well, fair enough, if they really do intend to think about it and not just make an excuse to leave. Nicodemus wasn't ready to commit either way, but he was willing to commit to fairness. "Let Jesus have his say, and I'll think about it" was his attitude, and he did. What conclusion did he finally come to? ***John 19:39*** shows Nicodemus at the tomb with the disciples, apparently a disciple himself.

What, then, are we to make of these diverse responses to Jesus? On opposite ends are the believers and the rejecters. But in between are plenty of confused people and thoughtful people who just want some time to decide. They all have potential; some are just late bloomers who can be won for Christ, maybe by you, if you are patient.

Sad Times, Happy Times

John 10:30-42

Jesus felt the full range of human emotions. At times, He was happy, even humorous. ***Matthew 22:24*** *ye swallow a camel* must have brought some laughter. Other times, He was sad. ***Isaiah 53:3*** *a man of sorrows acquainted with grief.*

Disciples who deserted Him made Him sad (***John 6:66-67***). A friend's grief made Him sad (***John 11:35***). And there was another time when He was very sad indeed. He was teaching a hostile crowd, hanging in there with them, teaching them despite their anger, because He loved them. He told them what they needed to hear, despite the great personal risk to Himself. And, despite their mounting anger, He said this to them:

> ***John 10:30*** *I and my Father are one.* ***:31*** *Then the Jews took up their stones again to stone him.* ***:32*** *Jesus answered them, Many good works have I shewed you from my Father; for which of those works do ye stone me?* ***:33*** *The Jews answered him, saying, For a good work we stone thee not; but for blasphemy; and because that thou, being a man, makest thyself God.*

It is sad when the truth makes people angry, sadder that it makes them angry enough to kill. And His point ("for which of those good works do want to kill me?") is right on the mark. He healed their lepers, their blind, their lame, and raised their dead. And now they wanted to kill Him. How ungrateful could they be? I believe He was shocked by their violent response.

How did He respond to their outrage? He could have said, "Forget I said anything," and walked away. But instead, He committed Himself further, confirming what He had just said, making them angrier still.

> ***John 10:34*** *Jesus answered them, Is it not written in your law, I said, Ye are gods?* ***:35*** *If he called them gods, unto whom the word of God came, and the scripture cannot be broken.* ***:36*** *Say ye of him, whom the Father hath sanctified, and sent into the world, Thou blasphemest; because I said, I am the Son of God?* ***:37*** *If I do not the works of my Father, believe me not.* ***:38*** *But if I do, though ye believe not me, believe the works: that ye may know, and believe, that the Father is in me, and I in him.*

Nothing could have made these people angrier—cold, hard facts that they could not argue with. Your own scriptures say you are gods, and yet you are stoning me for claiming God is in me. God sent me into the world; you can see that by my works, and yet you accuse me of blasphemy. Facts are facts, and they had no response except their stones.

Well, if doing all those wonderful things for them was not enough to persuade them, then there was nothing left to do but leave.

And so He did. He left. Not the street or the neighborhood, or the city, but the country.

> ***John 10:39*** *Therefore they sought again to take him: but he escaped out of their hand.* ***:40*** *And went away again beyond Jordan into the place where John at first baptized; and there he abode.*

Jesus had had enough. He was not immune to human feelings, and to nearly be killed for doing good seems to have brought him to despair. He left, and He left alone. There were no disciples with Him, no family, no entourage as befitting the Son of God, no caravan. He abandoned everything and returned alone to where it all began, where repenting Jews first came to Him and John in this desolate wilderness. It was still a desert where nothing grew. Had he accomplished anything at all since He had first left that place? The loneliness and the sadness must have been overwhelming.

But then, something good happened. Something that He might not have expected.

> ***John 10:41*** *And many resorted unto him, and said, John did no miracles; but all things that John spake of this man were true.* ***:42*** *And many believed on him there.*

It wasn't a waste after all. There were people who believed Him—His words and His works. And when they learned that He had fled to the desert, they followed him there.

Jesus wasn't completely alone. These people were true friends who came all the way out to that wasteland to find Him and be with Him. Maybe some who came had been in that crowd that tried to stone Him, and then thought it through: "You know what? He's right. God *is* in Him. The miracles prove that." And they spread the word, and they left their homes and their jobs, and they came.

Jesus had friends after all. It wasn't all hatred and violence; there were times of happiness for Jesus, and this was one of those times.

What made Jesus happy? The same things that make you and me happy: love, peace, and good friends.

One day, we will see Jesus. It will be a sad meeting if we've done things that made Him sad. But how wonderful it will be if He says to us, "Welcome, friend. You made me happy."

The Touchable Jesus

John 20:17

John 20:17 *Jesus saith unto* [Mary], *Touch me not; For I have not yet ascended to my Father…*

With everything else that we know about Jesus, it's hard to imagine that He could ever be untouchable. This verse in the King James version makes Jesus sound stand-offish, almost in a panic, demanding, "Don't touch me!" as if there is something wrong with His post-resurrected, pre-ascended body that's fragile and dare not be touched, like He's going to break.

There is a better interpretation that makes a whole lot more sense. Let's carefully examine the events of that first Easter morning.

Mary Magdalene and the other women came to the tomb early (***Matthew 28:1, Mark 16:1, Luke 24:10***). When they saw the open tomb, Mary ran to get Peter and John (***John 20:2***). The other women remained at the tomb, met angels, learned that Jesus had risen, then left. (***Matthew 28:5-8***). Mary returned to the tomb with Peter and John (***John 20:4***). The men left, leaving Mary alone at the tomb, weeping. That's when it happened, when the Lord came to Mary and said, "Touch me not." Cold words for one so dear as Mary. But that's not quite what He said, and we can see that by what happens next. The other women were still on the road.

> ***Matthew 28:9*** *And as they* [the other women still on the road] *went to tell his disciples, behold, Jesus met them, saying, All hail. And they came and held him by the feet, and worshipped him.*

Well, that's different. Is that significant? Yes, it is. Why? Because they touched Him. In fact, they were touching Him a lot, and this was only minutes after He left Mary at the tomb. I've heard some explain it as Jesus had just exited the tomb and could not be touched before he ascended to heaven. Are we to believe that during those minutes between meeting Mary and the women on the road, He rushed to heaven and rushed back? That, of course, would be nonsense. The ascension is the ascension, recorded later in ***Acts 1:9***. There is no other ascension, no pre-ascension.

So, what does it mean? The Greek word haptou [ἅπτου] means to cling to someone both physically and emotionally. So when Jesus said to Mary, "Touch me not," He didn't say, "Don't touch me." He said, "Mary, you need to let go. There are other people I need to see before I ascend." In other words, when Jesus said, "Touch me not," that is exactly what she was doing: touching Him, holding Him, clinging to her Savior whom she loved and had watched die, and I'm sure she was determined never to let Him go again.

When He appeared to her, and she responded, "Rabboni!" it probably only took her half a second to spring across the short distance that separated them. He probably could not have reflexed fast enough to hold her off and say, "Don't touch me." I believe she was all over Him before He could say or do anything to prevent her embraces.

The text, ***John 20:17***, is better translated as any of these:

"Do not cling to me"	New English Bible
"Stop clinging to me"	New American Standard
"Do not hold onto me"	New International Version

Any of those is a more accurate translation. In other words, "Mary, I must leave. You must let me go."

Isn't that a much sweeter picture, Mary clinging to him as he needs to go?

Jesus didn't keep people at arm's length. He touched people. He touched lepers (***Matthew 8:3***), and blind people (***Matthew 9:29***), and children (***Mark 10:13***), and Thomas (***John 20:27***). And, as always, with a touch, he healed (***Matthew 14:36***).

Does Jesus touch us today? Oh yes. In the most intimate way possible: He is in us and we in Him.

> ***John 14:20*** *At that day ye shall know that I am in my Father, and ye in me, and I in you.*

And you can't get any closer than that.

What Makes a Successful Mission?

John 3:26-36

From man's point of view, the mission of John the Baptist was a failure. He lost all of his followers and ended up dead. But from God's point of view, John's mission was a resounding success. Why? Because the success of a missionary's mission is measured not by how many people follow the missionary but by how many people follow Christ. John knew that.

John's disciples didn't agree with that, however, not at first. And when the crowd began to leave John and turn to Jesus, John's disciples came to him and complained.

> ***John 3:26*** *...behold...all men come to him.*

They were jealous for John's sake. "He's taking all your followers, John. What are you going to do about it?" Here's John's response:

> ***John 3:27*** *...A man can receive nothing, except it be given him from heaven.* ***:28*** *Ye yourselves bear me witness, that I said, I am not the Christ, but that I am sent before him.* ***:29*** *,,,the friend of the bridegroom...rejoiceth greatly because of the bridegroom's voice: this my joy therefore is fulfilled.* ***:30*** *He must increase but I must decrease.*

In other words, if people are leaving me and going to Him, that's fine with me because that's the way God wants it. Every missionary knows and declares that it's not about himself, it's about Christ. The missionary is simply a forerunner, a herald. What makes the missionary glad is to know that people have come to Christ, regardless of what happens to the missionary.

Here is John's testimony of Jesus:

John 3:31 *He…cometh from above…*
Jesus is from God.

John 3:32 *…what he hath seen and heard, that he testifieth…*
Jesus has seen and heard the real truth.

John 3:33 *…his testimony…that God is true.*
Jesus testifies of God's truthfulness.

John 3:34 *…he whom God hath sent speaketh the words of God:*
Jesus speaks God's words.

John 3:35 *…The Father…hath given all things into his hand…*
Jesus has all things that God has.

John 3:36 *…He that believeth on the Son hath everlasting life…*
Jesus gives everlasting life.

This is a powerful testimony that John gives of Jesus. No wonder John points to Jesus and says, "Follow Him, not me."

And people did. John's mission was a total success. May yours be as well.

Submitting to the King

John 6:15-66

Clearly, it is Christ's destiny to be king.

Genesis 49:10 *Until Shiloh come.* (Shiloh means "whose right it is to rule").

Isaiah 9:6 *The mighty God, the Everlasting Father, the Prince of Peace.*

Daniel 9:25 *Messiah the Prince*

Matthew 2:2 *...born King of the Jews.*

Matthew 21:5 *Behold, thy king cometh unto thee.*

John 18:37 *Art thou a king? To this end was I born.*

1 Timothy 6:16 *The only Potentate, the King of kings.*

But maybe the Bible doesn't mean king in any real earthly sense because Jesus said—

John 18:36 *My kingdom is not of this world.*

But that's only temporary because the Bible also says—

Revelation 11:15 *The kingdoms of this world are become the kingdoms of our Lord and of his Christ; and he shall reign forever.*

So eventually, at some unknown future time, Jesus will be the monarch of the world.

Here's a question: Why did Jesus decline to be king when the job was offered to him?

John 6:15 *When Jesus therefore perceived that they would come and take him by force, to make him king, he departed.*

Why didn't he jump at the chance? Why did he "depart"? Here's why:

John 6:26 *Ye seek me…because ye did eat.* ***:51*** *I am the living bread which came down from heaven: if any man eat of this bread he shall live forever: and the bread that I will give is my flesh.* ***:66*** *From that time many of his disciples went back, and walked no more with him*

That was a modern-thinking crowd. As long as Jesus was handing out free stuff, hey, make him king. He's got our vote. Much like today, many people vote for whoever promises the most goodies.

The early followers of Christ knew what entitlements were. But when He asked *them* to do something—"eat my flesh, drink my blood"; in other words, accept me on my terms, be what I am, commit yourselves to my life and my death—well, they didn't want to have anything to do with that. So, they left.

Total commitment, which Jesus was demanding of them, was, in their opinion, too much for a king to ask. "Feed us," and we're on board. But "commit to you," ah, no thanks. That's why Jesus could not be their king. They didn't want a king; they wanted free stuff, entitlements.

Is Jesus your king? That means more than accepting His gifts; it means coming on your knees in submission to His sovereign will.

Lazarus and the Death Conqueror

John 11:15-44

The subject of this story first appears to be Lazarus. But it is not. The subject of this story is Jesus, the Death Conqueror.

> ***John 11:15*** *Then said Jesus unto them, Lazarus is dead.* ***:16*** *...to the intent that you might believe.*

The reason Lazarus died was so they could believe.

Death is not our friend; it is our enemy. It is the result of sin (***Roman 6:23*** *The wages of sin is death*) and is the domain of Satan (***Hebrews 2:14*** *...him that had the power of death, that is, the devil*). Of all things, mankind most desperately needs someone to conquer death. If death is a good thing, then why did Jesus go through so much trouble to defeat it? Wouldn't we be content to die and stay dead if death is so good? Death is the enemy and something to defeat. That's why the resurrection.

Jesus' friends knew that He had amazing powers. He healed lepers, cast out devils, walked on water, and created food. Was there anything this man could not do? His friends loved Him and believed Him, but when Lazarus died, even their faith had limits.

> ***John 11:20*** *Then Martha...went and met him.* ***:21*** *If thou hadst been here my brother had not died.* ***:22*** *But I know whatsoever thou wilt ask of God, God will give it thee.* ***:24*** *I know that he shall rise in the resurrection.*

Martha stretched her faith forward one more step, then fell back. Maybe Jesus could raise Lazarus even now. But no, that's beyond even His abilities. Oh well. There will be a resurrection. It is a precious faith that seeks to believe what it dares not.

> ***John 11:40*** *Said I not unto thee that if thou wouldest believe, thou shouldest see the glory of God?* ***:42*** *…that they may believe that thou* (God) *hast sent me* ***:43*** *Lazarus, come forth!* ***:44*** *And he that was dead came forth.*

Everyone there saw the dead come forth. That was wonderful, nothing wrong with that. But a few, the believers, saw much more than a dead man come back to life: they saw the glory of God.

What you see depends on where you're looking. If you're looking at the dead man, when the dead arise, you see a living Lazarus. But if you're looking at Christ, when the dead arise, you see the living God, that creative being who made the worlds, now directing his power to deliver mankind from the jaws of death. That is what Martha saw and, hopefully, what we see on our Easter celebration.

Pharisees and Lepers

Matthew 8:1-3

Why did Jesus perform miracles? The simple answer, "because He loved people," doesn't do justice to the question. Maybe a better way to ask it is why did God have Jesus perform miracles? The answer to that question is what the Bible says, namely:

> ***Matthew 9:6*** *…that ye may know that the Son of man hath power on earth to forgive sins*
> ***John 5:36*** *The works that I do bear witness of me…*
> ***John 11:42*** *…that they may believe that thou hast sent me.*
> ***John 20:31*** *…that ye might believe…*

The Bible declares this so often that it's not debatable. The purpose of the miracles was as evidence that Jesus was who he said he was, and not merely to do kind things for people. Yes, Jesus loved people, but the kindest thing He could do for people was to save their souls, and that required a conspicuous declaration. And for that reason, He did miracles—so that people who saw them would believe.

Did it always work? Did people who saw the miracles always believe? Sometimes they believed, and sometimes they didn't. Pharisees, in particular, had a difficult time believing.

> ***Matthew 12:24*** *When the Pharisees heard it, they said, This fellow doth not cast out devils but by Beelzebub the prince of devils.*

What an odd conclusion. They didn't doubt the miracles; they just concocted an absurd explanation to avoid conceding anything to Jesus. Jesus had no place in their worldview and was a threat to their established positions. In other words, they had too much to lose and were therefore strongly motivated to reject Jesus.

Now, lepers, on the other hand, had nothing to lose. So that freed them to believe whatever the facts demanded of them. On the social ladder, no one was lower than lepers. They were not permitted in the camp (***Numbers 5:2***), and no one was permitted to touch them (***Leviticus 5:3***). Not only did they have to endure such a terrible disease, but also a terrible life-long loneliness as well. But despite the scorn and the rejection, lepers came to Jesus.

> ***Matthew 8:1*** *...great multitudes followed him* ***:2*** *And behold, there came a leper and worshipped him, saying, Lord, if thou wilt, thou canst make me clean.*

This leper came right through the crowd. Didn't he know that he wasn't supposed to be there?—that everyone hated him and would shout him away? Maybe they would throw rocks at him or hit him with sticks. Didn't he know that? Yes, he knew. But he also knew that his plight was desperate, and there was only one source of help. He didn't care what the crowd thought of him or even what the law said. He thought about only one thing: getting help from Jesus. And he got it.

> ***Matthew 8:3*** *And Jesus put forth his hand and touched him, saying, I will; be thou clean. And immediately his leprosy was cleansed.*

Jesus touched the untouchable. When we touch uncleanness, we become unclean. But when Jesus touched uncleanness, the uncleanness was cleansed.

This really speaks to motivation, doesn't it? Why were the lepers so accepting of Jesus while the Pharisees rejected Him? The answer can only be: It depends on what they had to gain or lose. If Jesus threatens your secure lifestyle, the motivation is to reject. But if Jesus holds your only hope for happiness, the motivation is to accept. It is a rare person who can set aside his personal situation and assess the truth based on facts alone. We are all similarly motivated. The trick is to arrive at a place where we realize that there is no hope without Jesus. Only then will we turn to Jesus.

For selfish reasons? Well, yes, of course. I am selfish enough to want eternal life, just as I am selfish enough not to want cancer. Selfish is a poor choice of words, but I know no other. We all make decisions for our own best interest. You can call that selfish or something else. But in any case, God has our best interest at heart, and He wants us to act in our own best interest; namely, He wants us to accept Jesus as our Savior, for there is no other. In that regard, we are on equal footing with the lepers, without hope. Actually, so were the Pharisees; they just couldn't see it so easily, though the truth was staring them in the face.

To be a bit fair to the Pharisees, there were some Pharisees who did accept Jesus. Nicodemus was one of them. They really were religiously motivated. On the other hand, not one Sadducee ever accepted Jesus. They were politically motivated.

Light

Matthew 5:14-16

Matthew 5:14 *Ye are the light of the world…*

It is said that the best way to teach is by example, and that may be true. The heart of any message is the example of the messenger. But if example is all there is to a message, then it's an incomplete message. The Christian message must always have two parts: what the Christian does and what the Christian says; the deeds and the words; or, as Jesus says here, salt and light.

Salt influences the world from within. Food is better with salt. The world is better when it has godly people. But light influences the world from without. Not by changing the world as salt does, but by exposing the truth so that the world will be motivated to change. Both are necessary.

Acts 1:1 *The former treatise have I made, O Theophilus, of all that Jesus began to both do and teach.*

Certainly, it is a mistake to teach a truth and not live it. That's hypocrisy. But it is also a mistake to live a truth and not teach it. That's, well, what exactly is that? Cowardice maybe? Or selfishness? That's like Jonah, who loved God's truth and thought it was just fine that Israel had God all to itself, and he was not at all interested in sharing God with those foreign Assyrians—until God introduced Jonah to a giant fish.

Jesus had a great deal to say about light.

Matthew 5:14 *…A city that is set on an hill cannot be hid.* ***:15*** *Neither do men light a candle, and put it under a bushel, but on a candlestick; and it giveth light unto all that are in the house.* ***:16*** *Let your light so shine before men, that they may see your good works, and glorify your Father which is in heaven.*

In ancient Israel, cities were typically built on hills. And at night, when people lit the lamps in their homes, travelers could see the glistening city afar off and go right to it.

Shouldn't the city of God be as conspicuous? And, if it is important for lights to be visible outside for travelers, isn't it at least as important for lights to be visible inside for "all that are in the house," so they don't stumble around in the dark, and trip, and hurt themselves?

Ephesians 6:4 *Bring* [your children] *up in the nurture and admonition of the Lord.*

Nurture and admonition simply mean what you do and what you say, salt and light, for your family, and for everyone else. Live the gospel, certainly. But do not neglect the preaching of it. Do not expect people, particularly your own children, to guess your beliefs. Tell them, so you'll know that they know. Notice also that God does not tell us to turn on the light; he has already done that. All he is asking of us is to "Let it shine."

2 Corinthians 4:6 *God, who commanded the light, to shine out of darkness, hath shined in our hearts, to give the light of knowledge of the glory of God in the face of Jesus Christ.*

Mary and Judas: Love Versus Hate

John 12:1-8

We tend not to talk about villains very much—their lives are too depressing. It's nicer to talk about heroes. But the bible says a lot about villains and with good reason. Mostly because the Bible is real history, and real history is practically spray-painted with villainy. But also because while God wants us to be good, he also wants us not to be bad, and so God not only gives us good examples to follow but also bad examples to not follow.

Judas is unique in history. While there are many who would betray a friend for money, only one had the distinction of betraying the very best friend the world ever had.

It was Saturday, the evening before Palm Sunday. Jesus was at the home of Simon the Leper in Bethany, enjoying supper and the company of good friends. Then Mary, Lazarus's sister, did a peculiar thing.

> ***John 12:3*** *Then took Mary a pound of ointment of Spikenard, very costly, and anointed the feet of Jesus and wiped his feet with her hair; and the house was filled with the odour of the ointment.*

Costly indeed. All the way from Tibet. A pound was worth three hundred pence. At a workman's wages of a penny a day, that was a year's salary she poured on Jesus. And she washed his feet! Only slaves wash feet. And the mess she made. Oh my. Look at that. Dripping on the floor. And she forgot a towel. Where's a towel? No towel. Quickly, without thinking, Mary unbundled her hair (a Jewish faux pas) and used her lovely hair to dry Jesus' feet.

Extravagant. Embarrassing. Where was her dignity? It was gone, replaced by uncontrolled love which cannot be measured in dollars and cents, and cares nothing for the opinions of party guests. But everyone was polite, everyone was kind. Except one.

Then Judas spoke and complained.

> ***John 12:4*** *Then said one of his disciples, Judas Iscariot, Simon's son which should betray him.* ***:5*** *Why was not this ointment sold for three hundred pence and given to the poor?* ***:6*** *This he said not because he cared for the poor; but because he was a thief and had the bag and bare what was put therein.* ***:7*** *Then said Jesus, let her alone: against the day of my burying hath she kept this.* ***:8*** *For the poor always ye have with you; but me ye have not always.*

Judas wasn't interested in the poor. He had other things on his mind: a dying Christ (There, Jesus said it again: He will die), a failed kingdom, three wasted years, and now how to bail out of it all without empty pockets. Three hundred pence from the wasted spikenard would have lined Judas's pockets nicely.

But it was the Lord's reproof that was Judas's tipping point. That reproof was the last straw. That very night, as everyone slept, Judas's anger and greed led him out of the house and to Jerusalem, where he arranged to trade his Lord's life for thirty pieces of silver.

The combination of hate and greed will do that to a man, lead him to violence and betrayal. But boundless love, such as Mary's, will bring us, on our knees, to the feet of the Savior.

Melchizedek: Picture of Christ, the Better Priest

Hebrews 7:1-12

When the message of Christ was preached to the Jews, a principal objection was priesthood. "But we already have a priest: Aaron. His priesthood brings us to God, so what need have we of yet another priest? Why Christ?"

That's a fair question. The short answer is that Christ's priesthood is "better." That, of course, is a tall claim, easy to say, harder to prove. So, let's prove it. The Hebrew scriptures (Old Testament) say this about the priesthood of the coming Christ:

> ***Genesis 14:18*** *Melchizedek king of Salem…was the priest of the most high God.* ***:19*** [Melchizedek] *blessed* [Abraham] ***:20*** *and* [Abraham] *gave* [Melchizedek] *tithes.*

> ***Psalms 110:4*** *…Thou art a priest for ever after the order of Melchizedek.*

That's it. Pretty scant, just four terse verses. But it says everything we need to know.

Here is the connection: The Psalms tell us that when Christ comes, his priesthood will not be the Jewish priesthood, Aaron's priesthood, but will be a different priesthood, Melchizedek's priesthood, a "better" priesthood. The reasoning is straightforward. If Melchizedek's priesthood is better than Aaron's priesthood, then Melchizedek is better than Aaron. And if

Christ comes with Melchizedek's priesthood, then Christ, like Melchizedek, is better than Aaron.

Why is this important? Hebrews tells us why.

[1] Melchizedek's Priesthood is Royal

> ***Hebrews 7:1*** *For this Melchisedec, king of Salem, priest of the most high God…*

Israel's kings were not priests, and Israel's priests were not kings. Those two duties (head of state and head of church) were separated after Moses. Joshua became the head of state (political leader) and Eliezer (Aaron's son) became the head of the church. So separation of church and state became official, and the two authorities went their separate ways, often conflicting.

Note that prophecy had nothing to do with it—both men were prophets. They had to be to correctly administer their offices. One prophet led the nation, another prophet led the church.

But Melchizedek was different. He was both king and priest. And Christ, when he comes, Psalms tells us, will be like that: king and priest, ruling men for God and presenting us to God.

[2] Melchizedek's Priesthood is Eternal

> ***Hebrews 7:3*** *Without father, without mother, without descent, having neither beginning of days, nor end of life; but made like unto the Son of God; abideth a priest continually.*

Thus, the man Melchizedek is a model for God's priesthood. In Genesis, there is no record of Melchizedek's birth or death. That doesn't mean that he wasn't born or that he didn't die. It just means that there's no record of either. Aaron, on the other hand, his birth and death are recorded in Exodus. So the picture is that Aaron's priesthood began and will end, while Melchizedek's priesthood never began and will never end. His is an eternal priesthood.

This is a requirement of Christ and his priesthood. Why? Because the salvation he brings is eternal. He doesn't bring us into God's presence only for us to be kicked out once the offering wears off. That was the problem of Aaron's priesthood—new sins required new sacrifices.

> ***Hebrews 7:27*** *Who* [Christ] *needeth not daily, as those high priests, to offer up sacrifice…for this he did once when he offered up himself* ***:28*** *For…the Son…is consecrated for evermore.*

Christ made one sacrifice, which resulted in one eternal salvation. The priesthood of Aaron could never do that; that's why his priests performed sacrifices over and over.

[3] MELCHIZEDEK'S PRIESTHOOD IS SUPERIOR

> ***Hebrews 7:6*** *But he whose descent is not counted from them received tithes of Abraham and blessed him.* ***:7*** *And…the less is blessed of the better.*

Here's the point: Abraham paid tithes to Melchizedek; therefore, Melchizedek is better than Abraham. Melchizedek blessed Abraham; therefore, Melchizedek is better than Abraham. And Melchizedek was certainly no descendant or ancestor of Abraham's, so there can be no claim of priesthood by parentage—one did not come from the other.

Now for a picky detail:

Hebrews 7:9 *And as I may so say, Levi also, who received tithes, payed tithes in Abraham.* ***:10*** *For he was yet in the loins of his father, when Melchisedec met him.*

What is that all about? Well, you see a Jew could argue that, yes, Abraham paid tithes to Melchisedek, and therefore Melchisedek was Abraham's superior. But that was Abraham, and Abraham was not a priest. But Levi, standing for the Levitical priesthood, wasn't there. Maybe if he had been there, he might not have paid tithes to Melchisedec. Maybe Levi was his equal.

Hebrews argues back: But he was there. Not born yet, but still in the loins of Abraham. Therefore, Levi, his descendants, and the Levitical priesthood submitted to Melchisedek.

[4] Melchizedek's Priesthood is Perfect

Hebrews 7:11 *If therefore perfection were by the Levitical priesthood…what further need was there that another priest should rise after the order of Melchisedec, and not be called after the order of Aaron?*

This final argument is airtight. If the Levitical priesthood were perfect, there would be no need for another priesthood, would there? That Christ brings with Him a different priesthood—newer, and older—that alone proves that there is something deficient about the Levitical priesthood. Therefore, when Christ comes, it is critical that He bring with Him a different priesthood, one that accomplishes the things that the Levitical priesthood could not do.

Isaiah's Messiah

Isaiah 53

Isaiah is the quintessential book of Messianic prophecy, the "go to" book for anyone interested in what God had to say about the coming Messiah. But why? Why Isaiah and not, for example, Samuel, or Elijah? Yes, there are scattered messianic prophecies before Isaiah, but not many. ***Genesis 3:15*** *…her seed* speaks of a conception without a man. ***Genesis 49:10*** *The scepter shall not depart from Judah* speaks of a future royalty from Judah. And there is ***Psalms 22:1*** *My God, my God, why hast thou forsaken me?* ***:8*** *He trusted on the Lord that he would deliver him: let him deliver him, seeing he delighted in him.* ***:18*** *They part my garments among them, and cast lots upon my vesture.* These are quoted by Matthew to point to Jesus as the Christ.

But taken all together (these plus a few more) are at best obscure, that is, until the actual Messiah does arrive and these verses find their object. Then we understand them.

But then there's Isaiah, upon whom suddenly God downloads a raft of divine information about one future man: the coming Messiah. And one is inclined to ask, why? Why that man, Isaiah, and why that time? Was it arbitrary, or did God have a purpose?

No, it was not arbitrary, and, yes, God did have a purpose. Here's how it unfolded.

Two critically important events had just occurred that threw the nation of Judah into a panic.

First: Judah's northern neighbor had just been taken captive by the Assyrians and their king Sargon II. And Judah knew that they were next on Sargon's hit list. Judah felt impending doom, and there was little they could do about it.

Second: Judah's king Uzziah had just died. Judah didn't have many good kings (Israel had none), but Uzziah was one of those few. Uzziah had been good for the nation. Under him, Judah prospered and enjoyed justice. Once only did he offend God, and that cost him greatly: he was stricken with leprosy. Ironically, that experience might have made him an even better king, knowing, as he had learned from personal experience, that you don't mess with God. The nation felt secure under Uzziah's rule, and when he died, the nation's confidence died with him.

Enter Isaiah. The nation was frightened. Uzziah was dead, the Assyrians were coming, what would become of them? At that moment of great alarm, while Judah was in a listening mood, God opened the heavens to human eyes, revealed Himself as the real king (not the dead leper Uzziah), and Judah did indeed have a bright and wonderful future, which included the coming world Savior, the Messiah.

> ***Isaiah 6:1*** *In the year that king Uzziah died I saw also the Lord sitting upon a throne, and lifted up, and his train filled the temple.* ***:2*** *Above it stood the seraphims: each one had six wings; with twain he covered his face, and with twain he covered his feet, and with twain he did fly.* ***:3*** *And one cried unto another, and said, Holy, holy, holy, is the Lord of hosts: the whole earth is full of his glory.*

This great, divine king who sat on His throne in heaven was in charge, not only of Judah's destiny, but the whole world's. And His power was unchallengeable because He was "holy, holy, holy." God is many things. He is light, He is love, He is truth—what He is not, however, is "light, light, light." Above all His attributes, His most important is holiness. He is not just holy,

He is "holy, holy, holy." God is so holy, in fact, that the angels needed to shield themselves from Him. They needed six wings. Two for flying, of course, but two more to cover their exposed feet and two more to cover their exposed heads.

In other words, God's essential being is holiness, apart from all sin and failure. He is so holy that being close to Him was a dangerous place to be. Why is that important? Because: a being that holy cannot fail; His word and His will are unchallengeable. In other words: Judah, trust Him.

And that is what Isaiah saw.

Well, that scared the willies out of poor Isaiah. Why? Because Isaiah was *not* holy.

> ***Isaiah 6:5*** *Then said I, woe is me!* [Cursed am I! Oie Ve!] *For I am undone; because I am a man of unclean lips, and I dwell in the midst of a people of unclean lips: for mine eyes have seen the King, the Lord of hosts.*

Isaiah had a problem. He had sin, and he was standing in the presence of the holy, holy, holy God who could not tolerate sin. Surely Isaiah would not survive. But then, a marvelous thing happened.

> ***Isaiah 6:6*** *Then flew one of the seraphims unto me, having a live coal in his hand, which he had taken with the tongs from off the altar:* ***:7*** *And he laid it upon my mouth, and said, Lo, this hath touched thy lips: and thine iniquity is taken away, and thy sin purged.*

This is simply amazing. Isaiah stood in the presence of the holy God and lived to tell about it. His sin was purged. By what? By the burning coal of an altar. By a sacrifice. What sacrifice? Isaiah was about to find out.

And what sins were purged? The sins of his mouth. Most of our sins are sins of our mouths, aren't they? Lying, anger, seduction—words that we speak that we ought not to speak. And why clean up Isaiah's mouth? Because God had use for Isaiah's mouth, and God's message would necessarily be a holy message, God needed Isaiah's mouth to be holy.

> ***Isaiah 6:8*** *Also I heard the voice of the Lord, saying, Whom shall I send, and who will go for us? Then said I, Here am I; send me.* ***:9*** *And he said, Go, and tell this people, Hear ye indeed, but understand not; and see ye indeed, but perceive not.*

God had a message for Judah, one that they wouldn't understand. But that's okay that they didn't understand it; it needed to be documented. And it was. It's called the Book of Isaiah. Something was big coming—bigger than big, bigger than Judah, bigger than Assyria, something huge. What? The coming salvation of the world—and that message was Isaiah's to deliver.

Alright then, let's lay it out, this message from God to Isaiah, from Isaiah to Judah, and from Judah to the world—this message of Isaiah's Messiah.

> ***Isaiah 7:14*** *Behold, a virgin shall conceive, and bear a son, and shall call his name Immanuel.*

Wow! Isaiah starts off big, doesn't he? A virgin-born son is coming, and His name will be "God with us!" In other words, God is coming here; He will be born!

But how can God come when He is already here? He is living in the temple above the Ark of the Covenant, isn't He? Well, yes, but a lot is going to happen between now and then.

Isaiah 9:6 *For unto us a child is born, unto us a son is given: and the government shall be upon his shoulder: and his name shall be called Wonderful, Counsellor, The mighty God, the Everlasting Father, The Prince of Peace.*

Everything there is critically important. God, the Everlasting Father, will be born. How in the world is that even conceivable, let alone possible? And He will be your defense attorney with God, and He will bring peace—that is, "reconcile" or "atone"—between man and God.

Isaiah 11:1 *And there shall come forth a rod out of the stem of Jesse, and a Branch shall grow out of his roots.*

God has not forgotten David. That Davidic Covenant still stands sure. ***2 Samuel 7:16*** *And thine house and thy kingdom shall be established for ever before thee: thy throne shall be established for ever.* This is David's eternal dynasty, the only eternal dynasty in the history of the world. Christ, when He comes, must inherit the throne of David as a biological descendant and legal heir of David. Now that's tricky, considering that Christ must be virgin-born. But God wants it tricky so there can be no pretenders. Only the real Messiah can fulfill it all.

Isaiah 40:3 *The voice of him that crieth in the wilderness, Prepare ye the way of the Lord, make straight in the desert a highway for our God.*

This foresees John the Baptist, of course. The coming king, like all kings, needs a herald, someone to announce that the king is arriving.

> ***Isaiah 42:1*** *Behold my servant, whom I uphold: mine elect, in whom my soul delighteth; I have put my spirit upon him: he shall bring forth judgment to the gentiles.*

Christ pleases God, and God upholds Christ, and Christ carries God's spirit with Him so that He does the miracles that He does. What is the "judgment" that Christ brings to the Gentiles? Is God judging and condemning the Gentiles for what they've done to the Jews? It could mean that, but I don't think that's the meaning. I think it means that God gave the law, its courts, and its justice and fair play to the Jews. And Christ will take that to the whole world. Actually, that would condemn the world, but with Christ's atonement, God's "judgment" will save the world.

The following text must be separated into its component pieces:

> ***Isaiah 53:1*** *Who hath believed our report? And to what is the arm of the Lord revealed?*

God went out of His way to persuade the people that Jesus was who He claimed to be: the Son of God, the promised Messiah. Jesus' miracles were God's "report." But the people didn't believe Him. ***John 12:38*** *Though he had done so many miracles yet they believed not on him.*

> ***Isaiah 53:2*** *For he shall grow up before him as a tender plant, and as a root out of a dry ground: he hath no form nor comeliness; and when we shall see him, there is no beauty that we should desire him.*

Christ appeared to be an ordinary man from an ordinary family with an ordinary life. There was nothing special about Him.

He was not born to celebrity status as a son of a king normally would be.

> ***Isaiah 53:3*** *He is despised and rejected of men; a man of sorrows, and acquainted with grief: and we hid as it were our faces from him; he was despised, and we esteemed him not.*

"Man of sorrows" because He, more than any other man, understood the pain caused by sin. A sinner becomes numb to sin, jaded by self-justification and constant exposure. Just as eyes adjust to bright light, a sinner excuses himself, desensitizes himself to escape the pain of guilt. But for a sinless person to experience sin, it must have been exquisite for Him to feel that which, until then, He had had no part of.

"Acquainted with grief" because, like anyone else, He was tempted by sin. ***Hebrews 4:15*** *…tempted as we are, yet without sin.*

> ***Isaiah 53:4*** *Surely he hath borne our griefs, and carried our sorrows: yet we did esteem him stricken, smitten of God, and afflicted.*

He took our sins and our sadnesses, and we called Him crazy for doing that. Wouldn't a person have to be crazy to take someone else's sickness, someone else's sin and guilt, someone else's sorrows for family failure, business failure, all failure? That would be a crazy person, a masochist—who would do such a thing? Only someone who loves beyond all human reason. It is extreme love, not craziness, that drives a person to sacrifice himself or herself for someone else, like a mother throwing herself in front of an oncoming car to save her child.

Isaiah 53:5 *But he was wounded for our transgressions, he was bruised for our iniquities: the chastisement of our peace was upon him; and with his stripes we are healed.*

The "chastisement of our peace." What is that? First of all, the KJV translates this incorrectly. The Hebrew word mū-sar [מוּסָר] actually means "the chastisement for…" which was corrected in the New King James Version and aligns more closely with all contemporary translations.

In Western society, a criminal is punished with prison time and sometimes execution, while in other, less civilized nations, they often face amputation or torture. The world calls that "justice" and "paying a debt to society." And once that debt is paid, there is peace, reconciliation, or atonement. For Isaiah, Christ's chastisement, His punishment, is what brought us peace.

Isaiah 53:6 *All we like sheep have gone astray; we have turned every one to his own way; and the Lord hath laid on him the iniquity of us all.*

And what was the crime that required chastisement? The "gone astray." The "every one to his own way." If Isaiah, that great and righteous man, stood guilty before God (***6:5***) and was terrified by judgment, are we not at least as guilty as he?

Isaiah 53:7 *He was oppressed, and he was afflicted, yet he opened not his mouth: he is brought as a lamb to the slaughter, and as a sheep before her shearers is dumb, so he openeth not his mouth.*

The eunuch in ***Acts 8:32*** was reading this verse when Philip found him and taught him. No wonder he was confused and needed someone to explain it to him. Philip compared Christ's torture and crucifixion to a young, innocent animal being led willingly to its brutal, bloody death, and he called this Jesus' humiliation.

> **Isaiah 53:8** *He was taken from prison and from judgment: and who shall declare his generation? For he was cut off out of the land of the living: for the transgression of my people was he stricken.*

"Cut off" means executed as a criminal. But He had committed no crime, so why was He executed? He was executed in place of other people who *were* criminals.

> **Isaiah 53:9** *And he made his grave with the wicked, and with the rich in his death; because he had done no violence, neither was any deceit in his mouth.*

"Made his grave" means "assigned a grave." This verse really means: "It was intended that He be buried with the wicked; that is, in a common grave. But He ended up being buried with the rich in His own private grave instead." In Jesus' time, the bodies of those who were crucified (criminals) were generally left to rot anonymously in a mass grave. These were the dregs of society. So, how could this future suffering Messiah make His grave with the wicked and the rich, since the rich and powerful in that society were given expensive, personal tombs? This verse was actually needful. The good news message had to have an empty tomb so the disciples could point to it and say, "See? The tomb is empty because He rose from the dead." God, thanks to Joseph of Arimathea, arranged the details precisely.

> **Isaiah 53:10** *Yet it pleased the Lord to bruise him; he hath put him to grief: when thou shalt make his soul an offering for sin, he shall prolong his days, and the pleasure of the Lord shall prosper in his hand.*

"…shalt make his soul an offering…" ***2 Corinthians 5:21*** *For he hath made him to be sin for us, who knew no sin…*

"…shall prolong his days…" How can you prolong someone's days when they're dead? Simple. You resurrect them so that they live forever. The New English Bible translates it this way: "The Lord healed him."

> ***Isaiah 53:11*** *He shall see of the travail of his soul, and shall be satisfied: by his knowledge shall my righteous servant justify many; for he shall bear their iniquities.*

"Justify"—in other words, "not guilty" in a court of law. Acquitted. That's the verdict you want, isn't it? Let's go all the way back to ***9:6*** *…Wonderful, Counsellor…The Prince of Peace.* He is your defense attorney and wins a verdict for you of "not guilty" thus reinstating peace between you and God. Isn't that what you want?

> ***Isaiah 53:12*** *Therefore will I divide him a portion with the great, and he shall divide the spoil with the strong; because he had poured out his soul unto death: and was numbered with the transgressors; and he bare the sin of many, and made intercession for the transgressors.*

After all is said and done, Christ is exalted to greatness, which is what He deserves. Why? Because He sacrificed His own soul for us to become and pay for our sins. ***Colossians 2:14*** *Blotting out the handwriting of ordinances that was against us…nailing it to his cross…*

And finally, there is this.:

> ***Isaiah 61:1*** *The spirit of the Lord God is upon me: because the Lord hath anointed me to preach good tidings unto the meek; he hath sent me to bind up the broken hearted, to proclaim liberty to the captives, and the opening of the prison to those that are bound.*

This is the verse that Jesus used to proclaim Himself, to put the world on notice that He had arrived. He stood in His own synagogue in Nazareth—they all knew who He was, the carpenter's son—and He read this verse to them (***Luke 4:18***) and declared that He, Himself, was the subject of the verse: ***Luke 4:21*** ...*This day is this scripture fulfilled in your ears.* There was no mistaking His meaning. He had claimed to be the Messiah, and they understood Him perfectly. That's why they tried to kill Him: ***Luke 4:19*** [They]...*led him unto the brow of the hill...that they might cast him down headlong.*

Here's the point: All of Isaiah's Messianic verses refer to one man, and that man is Jesus Christ. Jesus knew it and declared it to be so. We should also declare it to be so.

Miracles

The Gospels of Matthew and John

Do miracles convert people? Yes—and no. It depends. (Don't you love that hopelessly evasive answer, "It depends," which means nothing?) But it does, after all, depend on who is seeing the miracle.

There were many people who saw miracles and rejected God anyway. Pharaoh (***Exodus 10:12-20***). Pharisees (***Matthew 12:22-24***). False disciples (***John 6:26-30, 66***). Jesus was exactly right when he said, (***Luke 16:31***) *If they hear not Moses and the prophets, neither will they be persuaded, though one rose from the dead.* There are indeed some people (many people, actually) who will not be converted no matter what.

So are we to conclude that miracles don't convert people? No. The scriptures don't say that. There are people who came to Christ because they saw one or more of his miracles and believed. Nathaniel (***John 8:48-49***). Nicodemus (***John 3:2, 19:39***). Thomas (***John 20:27-28***). A healed blind man (***John 9:38***). A sincerely believing crowd (***John 10:41-42***). And of course, Paul, who encountered the resurrected Lord on the road to Damascus.

Miracles are important. It is a serious mistake to suppose they are not. When Jesus cast out devils, and some Pharisees concluded that he was demonic, he said to them—

> ***Matthew 12:24*** *All manner of sin and blasphemy shall be forgiven unto men: but the blasphemy against the Holy Ghost shall not be forgiven unto men.*

Jesus was in effect saying: I can forgive you for rejecting what I say, but I can't forgive you for rejecting what the Holy Ghost does, namely, the miracles. If they reject the visible, obvious, conspicuous, miraculous workings of God, then there is nothing left that God can do that might persuade them. It's not that they can't be forgiven, it's that they won't be forgiven.

[1] Why Miracles?

Why did Jesus do miracles?

> ***Luke 7:22*** *Then Jesus answering said unto them, Go your way, and tell John what things ye have seen and heard; how that the blind see, the lame walk, the lepers are cleansed, the deaf hear, the dead are raised, to the poor the gospel is preached.*

His point: "Of course, I am the expected one. Don't you see the miracles I am doing? Haven't you been paying attention?"

There is no doubt that, from God's perspective, we are to believe Jesus *because* of the miracles, *because* of the open display of divine power. To those who say, "miracles don't convert," they are cutting their faith off at the knees. Why would anyone even say such a thing? Anyone can claim to be Christ, and many do—***Matthew 24:5*** *For many shall come in my name, saying, I am Christ; and shall deceive many.* But only one came with real power, the real Christ, and He did not mind demonstrating that power.

> ***John 5:31*** *If I bear witness of myself, my witness is not true.* ***:36*** *But I have greater witness than that of John: for the works which the Father hath given me to finish, the same works that I do, bear witness of me, that the Father hath sent me.*

He needed a second witness, and He had a second witness. God's witness made it unarguably clear to all who saw and to all who would later believe (that's you and me) that Jesus is the Christ. Why do we believe it? Not because Jesus said so (anyone can say anything), but because God said so—in the miracles.

> ***Matthew 9:6*** *But that ye may know that the Son of man hath power on earth to forgive sins, Arise, take up thy bed, and go into thine house.*

> ***John 10:38*** *Ye believe not me, believe the works.*

> ***John 14:11*** *Believe me that I am in the Father, and the Father in me: or else believe me for the very works' sake.*

Believe what I say or believe what I do. I don't care which, as long as you believe.

> ***John 14:29*** *I have told you before it come to pass that when it come to pass ye might believe.*

> ***John 20:30*** *And many other signs truly did Jesus in the presence of his disciples, which are not written in this book.* ***:31*** *But these are written, that ye might believe that Jesus is the Christ, the Son of God; and that believing ye might have life through his name.*

> ***2 Corinthians 12:11*** *…in nothing am I behind the very chiefest apostles…* ***:12*** *Truly the signs of an apostle were wrought among you in all patience, in signs, and wonders, and mighty deeds.*

Here's a challenging question: If there were no miracles in the Bible, would you believe the Bible's claims that God is God and Jesus is the Christ?

Here's the honest answer: Of course not! Words are just words, and outrageous claims (such as "Thou art the Christ") are just madness. Unless, of course, God provides proof. And God did provide proof, and that proof is the miracles. The reason we believe God's words is because God did miracles. It's not the words that convince us, it's the miracles.

What exactly is it that we believe? That God operates miraculously in the world. Here's the point: Without miracles, there is nothing *to* believe, unless we're willing to pray to a rock. People do that. But the difference between rocks and the true and living God is that the true and living God does miracles, giving evidence that He is true and living. Without miracles, He might as well be a rock. Words and claims don't cut it. We believe God lives because He has proven it.

Yes, of course, different people react to miracles in different ways.

> ***John 11:45*** *Then many of the Jews which came to Mary, and had seen the things which Jesus did, believed on him.* ***:46*** *But some of them went their ways to the Pharisees, and told them what things Jesus had done.*

But just because some people choose not to believe doesn't mean that miracles don't convert. It just means that miracles convert some and not others.

When Jesus raised Lazarus, some people "believed on him" because they saw the miracle while others rushed off to snitch on him. But to focus on the snitches and conclude that "miracles don't convert" is unfair. Rather, we should focus on the people who *were* converted by the miracles. Without them—Peter, Andrew, Thomas, etc.—there would be no church.

[2] Faith Before Miracles?

While we're discussing Lazarus, consider this question: Does faith always precede miracles? In this case, whose faith might we be talking about? Martha's? Did Jesus raise Lazarus because of Martha's faith? No. She didn't believe Jesus would raise her brother, and she had the most faith of anyone present.

> ***John 11:39*** *Jesus said, Take ye away the stone, Martha…saith unto him, Lord, by this time he stinketh.*

In other words, "Open the tomb? Are you crazy?"

Well, if not Martha, then Mary perhaps?

> ***John 11:32*** *Then when Mary was come where Jesus was, and saw him, she fell down at his feet, saying unto him, Lord, if thou hadst been here, my brother had not died.*

Not Mary. She was a basket case. All that was on her mind was the overwhelming grief of losing her brother. She did believe that if Jesus had arrived sooner He could have healed Lazarus from his illness, but she did not even consider the possibility that Jesus would raise the dead.

Anyone else? The disciples perhaps? Nope. Thomas said—

> ***John 11:16*** … *Let us also go, that we may die with him.*

Thomas was sure they were all going to die. No one believed that Jesus would raise Lazarus. It wasn't on anyone's mind. Then why did He do it if no one had faith that He could?

> ***John 11:42*** *And I knew that thou* [God] *hearest me always: but because of the people which stand by I said it, that they may believe that thou hast sent me.*

Jesus raised Lazarus, not in response to other people's faith but of His own volition. Yes, God responds to faith, but we should allow God to do what He wants, when He wants. Jesus performed this miracle ***so that people would believe***. And it worked! People believed.

The idea that God only performs miracles in response to faith is ludicrous. Here is a list of God doing miracles just because we wanted to:

> ***2 Kings 4:16*** *And he* [Elisha] *said, About this season, according to the time of life, thou shalt embrace a son. And she said, Nay, my lord, thou man of God, do not lie unto thine handmaid.* ***:17*** *And the woman conceived, and bare a son at the season that Elisha had said unto her, according to the time of life.*

This woman not only didn't believe Elisha, she called him a liar. But she was blessed anyway because of her kindness to the prophet. This woman's lack of faith had nothing to do with it. Her kindness to Elisha was sufficient to move God.

> ***2 Kings 5:8*** *And it was so, when Elisha the man of God had heard that the king of Israel had rent his clothes, that he sent to the king, saying, Wherefore hast thou rent thy clothes? Let him* [Naaman the Syrian] *come now to me, and <u>he shall know that there is a prophet in Israel.</u>*

Naaman was not only not a believer, he was a Syrian military leader. The Syrians were Israel's enemies. And he happened to be a leper. But he lucked out in that one of his wife's servants was a girl from Israel, and she was a believer. She told him about Elisha and how he was a man of miracles, but even when he took the journey, Naaman still balked at the instructions Elisha gave him. The only reason he finally did as the prophet asked was because his servant said why not at least try? Naaman was rewarded for obedience, not for faith.

Let's face the obvious: God uses His miracles to prove His own existence and His power. Many Christians want to squirm out of that. Why, I cannot imagine.

> ***John 5:7*** *The impotent man answered him, Sir, I have no man, when the water is troubled, to put me into the pool: but when I am coming, another steppeth down before me.* ***:8*** *Jesus saith unto him, Rise, take up thy bed, and walk.* ***:13*** *And he that was healed wist not who it was…*

The impotent man did not have faith in Jesus, didn't even know who Jesus was. This was just an idle conversation between two strangers. But Jesus healed him anyway, just because He wanted to, from the kindness of His own heart. Jesus did not say to this man as He had to the Syrophenician woman, "thy faith hath made thee whole."

One could argue, I suppose, that he had faith in the troubled water, and that faith put him there at the place and time, and therefore in contact with Jesus. But that's a stretch and entirely misses the point of "faith precedes the miracle."

My point is this: While we're arguing in behalf of faith, let's not argue that point so sternly that we deprive God of His own volition, His ability and willingness to act whenever He is so inclined. He doesn't have to wait for us. He created the world before there was anyone here to believe it could be done.

Acts 3:5 *And he gave heed unto them, expecting to receive something of them.* ***:6*** *Then Peter said, Silver and gold have I none; but such as I have give I thee: In the name of Jesus Christ of Nazareth rise up and walk.*

Another verse that argues against the idea that faith precedes the miracle. This lame man didn't even know who Peter and John were. He certainly did not expect a healing. What he expected was a coin, a contribution of some kind; what he got was a miraculous healing simply because Peter, and God, wanted to do it.

The danger of believing that faith must always come first is that faith can be in the wrong thing. It can be in a rock. Pagans have faith; in fact, it must be a really strong faith to believe in a rock or a statue. Does that make my faith weaker because I insist that it be in the one true God who has proven Himself by His miracles? I reject blind faith. Blind faith can cause you to worship a rock. I prefer instead to stand with the poor father of a dead child who said to Jesus—

Mark 9:24 *…Lord, I believe; help thou my unbelief.*

And Jesus did indeed help that man's weak belief; he brought his child back to life.

But what about this next verse?

[3] SIGN SEEKING

Matthew 12:39 *…An evil and adulterous generation seeketh after a sign…*

That sure seems to mean that if you insist on proof, then you are a bad person. But if that is what it means, then how are we to understand this verse?

> ***John 20:25*** *...But* [Thomas] *said unto them, Except I shall see in his hands the print of the nails, and put my finger into the print of the nails, and thrust my hand into his side, I will not believe.* ***:27*** *Then saith* [Jesus] *to Thomas, Reach hither thy finger, and behold my hands; and reach hither thy hand, and thrust it into my side: and be not faithless, but believing.*

Are we to believe that Thomas was "an evil and adulterous generation" because he insisted on seeing for himself? Clearly, that was not the case. Why? Because Jesus graciously accommodated his request (actually his demand): "I must see, or I will not believe."

So, what's the difference? The evil and adulterous generation made a rhetorical demand. They were saying, "bet ya can't." They *had* seen his miracles and still refused to believe. They were demanding signs, not to believe, but so they could justify their unbelief. They were simply looking for a trick that Jesus could not do, then say, "Ahah! Can't do that one, can you?"

Thomas's unbelief was altogether different than that. His belief was real, but it was shattered by Jesus' death. And for Jesus to ask him to believe in the resurrection without proof, that was more than Thomas could muster. He wanted proof. And what did Jesus do? Jesus gave him proof. Jesus didn't chide Thomas for his unbelief, no accusation of "evil and adulterous generation." Thomas's faith needed proof; Jesus gave him proof, and Thomas believed.

If miracles don't convert, there is something wrong with the picture of Thomas and Jesus. But there is nothing wrong. Here's the truth: Miracles convert. Not all, but some, and some is far different from "miracles don't convert." Thank God for miracles and those who believe them.

[4] Do Miracles Convert?

But just to lock it in, for die-hards who insist that miracles do not convert, here is a list of people who were converted to the truth because they saw a miracle, believed the miracle, and devoted their lives to God. I'll also include people who saw miracles and would not believe.

> ***Judges 6:36*** *Behold, I will put a fleece of wool in the floor; and if the dew be on the fleece only, and it be dry upon all the earth beside, then shall I know that thou wilt save Israel by mine hand, as thou hast said.* ***:37*** *And it was so: for he rose up early on the morrow, and thrust the fleece together, and wringed the dew out of the fleece, a bowl full of water.* ***:39*** *And Gideon said unto God, Let not thine anger be hot against me, and I will speak but this once: let me prove, I pray thee, but this once with the fleece; let it now be dry only upon the fleece, and upon all the ground let there be dew.* ***:40*** *And God did so that night: for it was dry upon the fleece only, and there was dew on all the ground.*

Notice that God did not express annoyance or anger toward Gideon for his doubt and need for confirmation. What God seems to be after is not our blind faith but our willingness and longing to believe. God accepts that He needs to seek after us much more than we need to seek after Him. And He says as much. What He insists on, however, is a sincere response to His reaching. If we respond to His reaching with rejection, then He will stop reaching.

> ***2 Kings 5:17*** *And Naaman said…for thy servant will henceforth offer neither burnt offering nor sacrifice unto other gods, but unto the* LORD.

Naaman was an avowed non-believer. But when he was cured of leprosy, he became an avowed believer. To argue that miracles don't convert is absurd. Naaman, once cured of leprosy, was now a follower of the only God who is God.

> ***2 Kings 20:11*** *And Isaiah the prophet cried unto the* L*ORD: and he brought the shadow ten degrees backward, by which it had gone down in the dial of Ahaz.*

Did God move the earth backwards, or did He reset time back a bit, or did He do something else? Whatever He did to pull this off, God demonstrated an awesome power over the universe and its laws. What's also interesting was his motive, almost trivial, to convince a man that God had extended his life by fifteen years.

> ***Luke 8:38*** *Now the man out of whom the devils were departed besought him that he might be with him…*

This man, cured of devils, became Jesus' instant disciple.

> ***Luke 16:31*** *And he said unto him, If they hear not Moses and the prophets, neither will they be persuaded, though one rose from the dead.*

I'm including this verse because there is a perfect contrary example: namely, Saul of Tarsus. Saul had exactly this experience. He was a non-believer, and one from the dead came to him, and Saul believed. So it cannot be generally true that "neither will they be persuaded, though one rose from the dead."

> ***Luke 17:15*** *And one of them, when he saw that he was healed, turned back, and with a loud voice glorified God.*

This miracle, the healing of the ten lepers, makes my point exactly. Yes, nine of the ten were ungrateful and didn't "convert," but one of them did. So the oft-touted claim that miracles don't convert is a false claim. True, miracles don't convert everyone, or even most. But miracles do convert *some*, actually many, and that is my point, that is *the* point, the reason that God does them, to find and save those few who see *and believe.*

> ***John 1:48*** *Nathanael saith unto him, Whence knowest thou me? Jesus answered and said unto him, Before that Philip called thee, when thou was under the fig tree, I saw thee.* ***:49*** *Nathanael answered and saith unto him, Rabbi, thou art the Son of God; thou art the King of Israel.*

Was this a big miracle? As miracles go, it was probably a small one. But big or small, it was enough to convince Nathanael. He became a lifelong disciple of Jesus. So don't tell me that miracles don't persuade. Nathanael would argue with you.

> ***John 2:23*** *Now when he was in Jerusalem at the Passover, in the feast day, many believed in his name, when they saw the miracles which he did.* ***:24*** *But Jesus did not commit himself unto them, because he knew all men.*

Yes, they believed because they saw the miracles. That was the point of the miracles.

But, if you are paying attention, you will complain: "Ahah. Most of them didn't continue to believe when things got tough," and you would be right. Most fell away, but not all. Some committed their lives to Jesus, and those "some" are what the miracles were all about. To say that miracles do not convert is simply not true, and we should stop saying that.

The reason people insist that "miracles don't convert" is because *they can't do miracles themselves*, plain and simple. And because they can't do them, they feel pressure to head off the hypocritical demand "show me a miracle and I will believe." So they dismiss the importance of miracles with a wave of the hand, "Ah, what's the big deal about miracles anyway? They're not so important. They don't convert anyone."

Miracles *are* important, and they *do* convert. They are God's way of revealing Himself to the world, whether the world believes or not. And for believers to dismiss the miracles as unimportant is as much a sin as non-believers rhetorically demanding a sign. If you can't perform miracles, fine. I can't either. But don't dismiss God's finest work as unimportant when they are actually critically important. The truth is, if it weren't for the miracles, there'd be nothing to believe *in*. We believe in God *because* He revealed Himself to the world by His conspicuous displays of power. Without that, we might still worship, but we'd be worshipping stones and idols! Or some smooth-talking charlatan.

Make no mistake about it. The reason, *the* reason, we worship the true and living God and not a rock is because of His conspicuous displays of power, which we call miracles, which the rock and the charlatan cannot do. God's power on display as recorded in the scriptures is the arrow that directs our faith towards him and away from the rock.

Miracles are the tiebreaker. To anyone who insists that miracles don't convert, they should try worshipping a rock. Most ancient civilizations did. You don't need miracles to worship a rock.

John 3:2 *...no man can do these miracles that thou doest, except God be with him.*

That's exactly the point! Nicodemus got it.

> ***John 4:48*** *Then said Jesus unto him, Except ye see signs and wonders, ye will not believe.*

This is not an accusation but a statement of fact. Jesus is exactly right. It is, in fact, the miracles that we believe, and therefore we believe God. Were it not for the miracles, why would we? Words are just words. Anyone can spout philosophy. Only God can do miracles.

> ***John 4:53*** *So the father knew that it was at the same hour, in the which Jesus said unto him, Thy son liveth: and himself believed, and his whole house.*

Don't tell me that miracles don't convert. One miracle, a risen dead son, converted this man and his whole house.

> ***John 6:30*** *They said therefore unto him, What sign shewest thou then, that we may see, and believe thee? What dost thou work?*

This has got to be the most frustrating text in the entire Bible. "Convince us. Show us a sign."

The day before, Jesus had performed one of the most visible miracles of His ministry: He fed thousands on just a few loaves of bread and fishes. The next day, the people returned, demanding another miracle. What had they just witnessed? Were they not watching? Not paying attention? Of course, they were paying attention. That's why they had returned, for more free food. These are what Jesus calls sign-seekers. Understand: A sign-seeker is not a person who wants a sign, but a person who will not believe the signs given and so demands another and another, refusing to believe, looking for an excuse to justify their unbelief. "Bet you can't do this, bet you can't do that." Jesus was very free with his miracles. The problem was not that they wanted His miracles (He wanted them to want His miracles), but that they refused to arrive at the obvious conclusion that He was the Son of God.

> ***John 6:26*** *Jesus answered them and said, Verily, verily, I say unto you, Ye seek me, not because ye saw the miracles, but because ye did eat of the loaves, and were filled.*

Let's consider the verse carefully because it dispels a false idea. That false idea is this: that we should not base our faith on the miracles. That is absolutely wrong. If our faith is not based on the miracles, then what should it be based on? Words? Jesus just had a debate about that very thing: you can't trust words—that's exactly the point he made in ***John 5:31-34***. Therefore, I show you miracles, which you can and must trust.

In ***:26***, Jesus affirms that to us again. Not only is it not true that we shouldn't trust miracles (a triple negative, sorry, but it's the only way to say it), He says so—He *wants* us to trust the miracles, and He complains: "Ye seek me, not because ye saw the miracles…" That's his complaint against them. He wanted them to believe him because he did miracles, but instead, they just wanted the free food.

> ***John 6:36*** *But I said unto you, That ye also have seen me, and believe not.* ***:37*** *All that the Father giveth me shall come to me; and him that cometh to me I will in no wise cast out.*

Yes, there are lots of people who have seen miracles and will not believe. But some will. There are a few who see miracles, believe them, and stay. So don't tell me that miracles don't convert.

> ***John 9:38*** *And he* [the healed blind man] *said, Lord, I believe. And he worshipped him.*

This blind man, whom Jesus healed, not only believed in Jesus and followed him but also defended him (***John 9:25-30***).

> ***John 10:32*** *Jesus answered them, Many good works have I shewed you from my Father; for which of those works do you stone me?* ***:33*** *The Jews answered him, saying, For a good work we stone thee not, but for blasphemy; and because that thou, being a man, makest thyself God.*

In other words, they saw the miracles but would have stoned Him anyway because they didn't like what He said. So do we conclude that miracles don't convert? Let's check the aftermath. Jesus fled to the desert to be alone. But He wasn't alone for long.

> ***John 10:41*** *And many resorted unto him, and said, John did no miracle: but all things that John spake of this man were true.* ***:42*** *And many believed on him there.*

These people saw the miracles, saw that Jesus did exactly what John said he would do, went through a lot of trouble to go to Him in a very hostile desert, and believed.

Did miracles convert these people? Yes. The miracles are exactly what converted them.

So, what must we conclude? We conclude that miracles convert some people, and miracles don't convert others. We must also conclude that the notion that miracles don't convert is false.

John 11:45 *Then many of the Jews which came to Mary, and had seen the thing which Jesus did, believed on him.* ***:46*** *But some of them went their ways to the Pharisees, and told them what things Jesus had done.* Some saw and believed; some saw and didn't believe.

John 12:11 *Because that by reason of him* [Lazarus] *many of the Jews went away, and believed on Jesus.*

It's undeniable. The raising of Lazarus brought many converts to Jesus.

John 12:37 *But though he had done so many miracles before them, yet they believed not on him:*

Who is the "they"? Not everyone believed.

John 20:28 *And Thomas answered and said unto him, My Lord and my God.*

Before Thomas saw and touched the risen Lord, he would not believe; he said as much. When he saw and touched, he not only believed but concluded that Jesus was both Lord and God.

John 20:31 *But these are written, that ye might believe that Jesus is the Christ, the Son of God; and that believing ye might have life through his name.*

To those who still insist that miracles don't convert, John's parting shot is that the point of the miracles is to make us believe and have eternal life. Without the miracles, and especially Christ's resurrection, just what is there *to* believe? What we believe is that God had displayed his power conspicuously through Jesus, and therefore there is a God and His Son. The miracles are *why* we believe. If it's just words, then it's just a story. It's the miracles that make it real.

> ***Acts 1:1*** *...all that he said and did.*

The apostles preached two things: what Jesus said and what Jesus did. What Jesus said was His salvation message. What Jesus did was His miracles, which proved his salvation message.

> ***Acts 1:3*** *...many infallible proofs...*

For those who still think the miracles are no big thing, from God's perspective, they are a very big thing. The miracles are the evidence that Jesus is who He claims to be.

> ***Acts 9:6*** *And he trembling and astonished said, Lord, what wilt thou have me to do?*

One man stricken blind, one restored vision, and one life-long conversion. Don't tell me that miracles don't convert. Saul didn't need to be told twice that he was on the wrong side; he immediately gave his life to Jesus and never wavered.

Now, a different story is told about Simon the sorcerer ***Acts 8:9***. Simon saw Peter's miracles and (although the entire story is not told in the Bible) became an enemy of the church. So, again the definitive answer to the question "do miracles convert?" is: some yes and some no. But that is far different than the thoughtless answer that miracles don't convert, when the scriptures are replete with examples to the contrary. When I hear such boneheaded stupidity in church, I have to sequester my impulse to stand and scream, "Does anybody bother to read the scriptures?"

> **Acts 9:40** *But Peter…said, Tabitha, arise. And she opened her eyes…* **:42** *And it was known throughout all Joppa; and many believed in the Lord.*

How clearer can it be? Peter raised one woman from the dead, and lots of people join the church—unless you believe that over time they all left the church, which would be nonsense.

> **Acts 13:11** *And now, behold, the hand of the Lord is upon thee, and thou shalt be blind…* **:12** *Then the deputy, when he saw what was done, believed, being astonished at the doctrine of the Lord.*

A negative miracle (harms rather than heals), but still a miracle. And the deputy believed.

> **Acts 14:9** *The same heard Paul speak: who stedfastly beholding him, and perceiving that <u>he had faith to be healed</u>,* **:10** *Said with a loud voice, Stand upright on thy feet. And he leaped and walked.*

Certainly, faith calls down the healing power of God. I never said it doesn't. I'm saying that God is free to act with or without your faith, but faith does influence him.

[5] The Basis of True Faith

It is the miracles that are the root of our faith. Admit it. But many will argue, no, the Holy Spirit is the root of our faith. I argue back, no, the Holy Spirit is the conviction of our faith, to actually believe. But to believe in what? Without the miracles, there is nothing to believe *in.* You can believe in a rock, but what good does that do? Faith in the wrong object is useless, and worse, it is dangerous. It is the miracles that point our spirit-driven faith to the right object: the true and living God, who proves to us by His miracles that He is who He says He is.

Let's have a little debate before I let you go. I'll ask the questions, and I'll provide the answers. Your job is to decide if you agree with my answers or not.

What do you believe?
That Jesus is the Messiah and the Son of God.

Good. Why do you believe that?
I read the scriptures, and the Spirit convinced me.

Convinced you of what?
That Jesus is…

You said that already. Why?
Because I believe what He said about himself.

But anyone can say anything.
But He did good works.

Lots of people do good works.
But His works were special.

How so? Why were His special?
Because (sigh) His works were miraculous.

You believe He did miracles?
Yes. And He rose from the dead.

That's why you believe His words?
Yes. In particular, His claims about Himself.

And if He hadn't done miracles?
Then I don't know that I could believe His words.

So His miracles converted you?
Yes, I suppose they did.

That is an honest assessment of Jesus, His life, His claims, and why we believe everything He said. If you agree, then never again say that miracles don't convert. They converted you.

The Place to Be

Matthew 14:22-28

Matthew 14:22 *And straightway Jesus constrained his disciples to get into a ship and go before him unto the other side while he sent the multitude away.*

Jesus gave them a direct command. "Leave." What did they do? They left. They got into a ship, leaving Jesus behind, and headed for the other side. That's obedience.

The conflicting thing about obeying God is that doing what He says may get you into trouble. And so it was with them. However, trouble or not, being where God tells you to be is still the safest place to be. Again: and so it was with them.

Matthew 14:24 *But the ship was now in the midst of the sea, tossed with waves; for the wind was contrary.*

Now that's trouble. Imagine that. They did exactly what Jesus told them to do, and now they were in trouble. The storm was more than trouble; it was life-threatening, and it worked against them, pushing them back, away from their destination.

But still, ***John 6:19*** *they rowed forward.* Why? Because they were determined to do what Jesus had told them to do, even though it was hard and dangerous. They were in a storm. But they were also in the place of obedience, which was the safest place to be, although it didn't feel so safe, surrounded by threatening waves. They had always felt safe with Jesus, but Jesus wasn't there and not likely to show up. They must have wondered, "Why did He send us out into this?" And all they could do was struggle with His command and do their best, even though it seemed fruitless and they were likely to perish.

Yes, obedience creates trouble, but obedience also earns God's protection.

> ***Matthew 14:26*** *And in the fourth watch of the night Jesus went unto them, walking on the sea.* ***:27*** *Saying, Be of good cheer; it is I: be not afraid.*

Even in the storm, it turned out, they were safe. Here is some very good advice: ***Jude 21*** *Keep yourself in the love of God.* Obedience does that. It keeps you in God's love and in His protection.

Peter, it seems, wanted to be even closer.

> ***Matthew 14:28*** *And Peter answered him and said, Lord, if it be thou, bid me come unto thee on the water.*

And Jesus did.

Why did Peter do that? Why did Peter ask Jesus to let him walk across the water? Did Peter do that to show off? No. Did he do it to test Jesus? No. He did it for the most compelling reason of all: safety. In that situation, Peter knew one thing above all else: In the midst of a storm, there is one guaranteed safe place to be, standing next to Jesus.

Final note. Who sees the miracles? Those who obey Jesus and endure the storm.

The Divine Power of Jesus

Matthew 8-9

Jesus did miracles. There's no doubt about that. But so did the prophets, a few of them anyway. Moses, Joshua, Elijah, Elisha, and others demonstrated God's power on earth.

But what impresses us about Jesus' miracles, far beyond the miracles of the prophets, is the scope of His power. The prophets, with God's intervention, controlled some things. Jesus, on the other hand, controlled everything.

Here then is the short list of the universal power that Jesus had and used:

[1] JESUS HAS POWER OVER DISEASE

> ***Matthew 8:2*** *And behold, there came a leper and worshipped him, saying, Lord, if thou wilt, thou canst make me clean.* ***:3*** *And Jesus put forth his hand, and touched him, saying, I will; be thou clean. And immediately his leprosy was cleansed.*

The Jews were forbidden to touch any unclean person (***Leviticus 5:3***). That was wise counsel from God. The idea of quarantine protected the people from the spread of contagion. If you touch uncleanness, you become unclean.

But Jesus touched these lepers without fear of contamination. Why? Because when he touched uncleanness, the uncleanness went away. Disease didn't affect Him; He affected the disease. He cured disease with a touch. Jesus had power over illness and the human body.

[2] JESUS HAS POWER OVER NATURE

Matthew 8:24 *And, behold there arose a great tempest in the sea, insomuch that the ship was covered with the wave: but he was asleep.* ***:25*** *And his disciples came to him and awoke him saying, Lord, save us: we perish.* ***:26*** *And he saith unto them, Why are ye fearful, O ye of little faith? Then he arose and rebuked the winds and the sea and there was a great calm.* ***:27*** *But the men marveled, saying, What manner of man is this, that even the winds and the sea obey him!*

That's a fair question. Indeed, what manner of man is this who tells the winds and the sea what to do, and they obey Him? Jesus has power over the natural world.

[3] JESUS HAS POWER OVER THE SUPERNATURAL ("SUPER"-NATURE)

Matthew 8:28 *And when he was come to the other side into the country of the Gergesenes, there met him two possessed with devils, coming out of the tombs, exceeding fierce, so that no man might pass by that way.* ***:29*** *And, behold, they cried out, saying, What have we to do with thee, Jesus, thou Son of God? Art thou come hither to torment us before the time?* ***:30*** *And there was a good way off from them an herd of many swine feeding.* ***:31*** *So the devils besought him, saying, If thou cast us out, suffer us to go away into the herd of swine.* ***:32*** *And he said unto them, Go. And when they were come out, they went into the herd of swine: and behold, the whole herd of swine ran violently down a steep place into the sea, and perished in the waters.*

An interesting note here is that devils know what most people don't know: that Jesus is the Son of God: ***James 2:19*** *…the devils* *also believe and tremble.* They also know that their time isn't up yet and negotiated that fact with Jesus.

Now, what about the pigs? Why pigs? Well, without the pigs, we might wrongly conclude that what Jesus is dealing with here is simply a mental disorder, insanity, crazy lunatics. But that cannot be, because the devils moved from humans to animals, who then drowned. So, what Jesus faced here were, quite literally, devils—sentient, malicious beings from an unseen world against whom we are helpless. And Jesus has power over them, over the supernatural world.

[4] JESUS HAS POWER OVER SIN

> ***Matthew 9:2*** *And, behold, they brought to him a man sick of the palsy, lying on a bed: and Jesus seeing their faith said unto the sick of the palsy; Son, be of good cheer; thy sins be forgiven thee* ***:3*** *And behold certain of the scribes said within themselves, This man blasphemeth.* ***:4*** *And Jesus knowing their thoughts said, Wherefore think ye evil in your hearts?* ***:5*** *For whether is easier, to say, Thy sins be forgiven thee; or to say, Arise, and walk?* ***:6*** *But that ye may know that the Son of man hath power on earth to forgive sins, (then saith he to the sick of the palsy,) Arise, take up thy bed, and go unto thine house.* ***:7*** *And he arose, and departed to his house.*

Here's the bad news: we sin. It's bad enough that we get sick and die, but that we are at odds with God's will is even worse. Here's the good news: Jesus has power to forgive sin. Isn't it interesting that they resented it! You can make some people mad simply by forgiving them.

Also interesting is that the healing was secondary to the forgiving. Why did Jesus heal? Because he loved people, certainly. But His love moved Him to do something far greater for us than heal our frail and dying bodies; His love moved Him to forgive us. He loved enough to heal, but more than that, He loved enough to forgive. The healing was simply the evidence that He *could* forgive, and would.

His ability to forgive is one thing; His willingness to forgive is another. To forgive, He had to pay a horrendous price. When He forgave this palsied man, He knew that He took on an outstanding debt that He was going to have to pay for. And that is exactly what He did. Jesus had power over sin.

[5] JESUS HAS POWER OVER DEATH

> ***Matthew 9:18*** *When he spake these things unto them, behold, there came a certain ruler, and worshipped him, saying, My daughter is even now dead: but come and lay thy hand upon her, and she shall live.* ***:19*** *And Jesus arose, and followed him, and so did his disciples.* ***:23*** *And when Jesus came into the ruler's house…* ***:25*** *…he went in, and took her by the hand, and the maid arose.*

In our moments of greatest desperation, we give up caring about trivial things like social status. This man was a ruler. He might not have spent a lot of time mixing with the common people, but when his daughter died, he wanted only one thing: to get to Jesus. He pushed to the front of the crowd, and in full view of everyone, he worshipped and pleaded for his daughter. Rulers don't do that, but this one did.

And what was Jesus' response? "Let's go." Whatever he was doing at that moment, He was willing to drop everything to go with this man to rescue his daughter.

This story reveals two things about Jesus: (1) He is willing to help and wants to right now. And (2) He can help, to the point of bringing the dead back to life. Think about that. Divine, life-restoring power can be turned to benefit you. Why would anyone not go to Him, and worship, and plead for what He so willingly wants us to have and gives so freely? Jesus has power over death.

[6] Summary

Jesus demonstrated that He has divine power. But much more than that, he demonstrated that he has *all* power. ***Matthew 28:18*** *…All power is given unto me in heaven and in earth.* He controls everything: your health, the earth, demons and angels, even sin, and finally your life, death, and new life again. As He said, ***John 16:15*** *All things that the Father hath are mine…* And He proved it.

Jesus Christ: Priest and King

Psalms 110:4

Israel had priests and kings, spiritual leaders and political leaders. But the priests were not kings, and the kings were not priests. Moses was both, that is, in the sense that he was both Israel's spiritual leader and political leader, head of the church and head of state.

After Moses, those two roles diverged. The head of the church was Aaron's son Eleazar, and the head of state was Joshua. They were both prophets receiving their directions from God, but that's not the point. The point is that one was a secular leader and the other a religious leader.

Then came the judges and finally the kings, and while a few were also prophets (Gideon and Deborah), they all acted only as secular leaders. The priests, on the other hand, were the head of their temple, their synagogues, and their religion. The priests brought men to God, and the kings ruled men for God. Basically, Israel had a distinct separation of church and state.

But what about Messiah? When He comes, what is He supposed to be? A priest? A king? Both? Neither? What? Here's the what:

Psalms 110:4 *Thou are a priest forever after the order of Melchizedek.*

When Messiah comes, He will certainly be a priest. But unlike Aaron, His priesthood will be like Melchizedek. So, what do we know about Melchizedek?

> ***Genesis 14:18*** *And Melchizedek king of Salem brought forth bread and wine: and he was the priest of the most high God.*

The important thing to know about Melchizedek was that he was a priest *and* a king. That's different than any of the leaders of Israel. If Messiah is after the order of Melchizedek, then He too must be a king and a priest, bringing men to God and ruling men for God.

Now to the point.

Jesus Christ is that Messiah, and his name indicates that.

Eusebius, in his 4th century work, *The History of the Church*, makes this compelling argument: He points out that the name "Jesus" is the Greek form of the Hebrew name "Joshua" (Yeshua), like the Joshua of old, the first secular leader of Israel. Indeed, our English Bibles even confuse those two English words: ***Hebrews 4:8*** *For if Jesus* [meaning Joshua] *had given them rest…* Indeed, in their gospels, both Matthew and Luke go to great lengths to establish Jesus' Davidic lineage, which made him a rightful heir to the Israelite throne.

Eusebius then points out that the name "Christ" is the Greek translation for the Hebrew word "Messiah," meaning "anointed," which refers specifically to the priests of Aaron (***Leviticus 4:5, 4:16, 6:22***).

So we see then that the name Jesus Christ presents Him to us as Joshua Messiah, meaning head of state and head of church, converging again, for the first time since Moses, both roles in one person.

But Jesus Christ is no ordinary political leader. He is not merely a judge (although He is that), He is a king, a priest/king with absolute authority on earth and in heaven. That's the Messiah we call Lord.

Hebrews 4:14 *a great high priest, Jesus the son of God*
Revelation 19:16 *King of kings, and Lord of lords*
Revelation 1:6 *And he hath made us kings and priests unto God*

The Curse of Coniah

Jeremiah 22:24, 30

All Jews and Christians know that when Messiah comes, He must be a reigning king of the house of David.

> ***Jeremiah 23:5*** *Behold, the days come, saith the* LORD, *that I will raise unto David a righteous Branch, and a king shall reign and prosper, and shall execute judgment and justice in the earth.*

A wonderful promise, and that is exactly what the ancient Jews expected. For instance, the New Testament begins with this:

> ***Matthew 1:1*** *The book of the generation of Jesus Christ, the son of David, the son of Abraham.*

The title "son of David" expressed the grand expectation of Jewish hope that the dynasty of David would reemerge and lead the nation to greatness. Actually, that did happen, but there was nothing simple or straightforward about how it happened. The biggest show-stopper was "the curse," specifically, the curse of Coniah, which, I'm sure, caused many Jewish scholars to scratch their heads and ask, "How can this ever happen?"

So, for your reading pleasure, here is the curse of Coniah:

> ***Jeremiah 22:24*** *As I live, saith the* LORD, *though Coniah* [or Jeconiah, or Jehoiachin, all the same person] *the son of Jehoiakim king of Judah were the signet on my right hand, yet would I pluck thee hence.* ***:30*** *Write ye this man childless, a man that shall not prosper in*

his days: for no man of his seed shall prosper sitting upon the throne of David, and ruling any more in Judah.

Ouch! The Davidic dynasty was done, meaning that no dynastic heir would ever actually reign. Oh, there will be dynastic posterity, but no one who has the right to reign will ever reign.

But how could that be? We just read ***Jeremiah 23:5*** *…I will raise unto David a righteous branch and a king shall reign…* So, what's the deal here? "A king shall reign from David," yet "no king shall reign of the kingly line." Sounds like a contradiction to me. How can the Messiah, the true Messiah, ever pass that test?—be a son of David, a dynastic heir with the right to reign, but avoid the curse that says He can never reign. Perplexing, isn't it?

A possible solution might be found in Zedekiah, a nephew who reigned after Jeconiah, and was the last king of Judah. He avoided the curse because he was not Jeconiah's son. But Zedekiah's sons were all killed (***2 Kings 25:7***), so Zedekiah is no help. No dynastic heirs there. This points us back to the problematic question: How can Messiah be in the royal line with the right to rule yet not be descended from the royal line so that he can rule? The answer is: adoption.

Matthew 1:12 *Jeconias begat Salatiel* [etc.]…***:16*** *And Jacob begat Joseph the husband of Mary, of whom was born Jesus who is called Christ.*

According to Matthew, Joseph was a descendant of Jeconias. He inherited the right to rule, but he also inherited the curse that he would never rule. But Jesus, adopted by Joseph, inherited the dynastic right to rule (he was the eldest of Joseph and Mary) but avoided the curse. Joseph was not Jesus' biological father, but he was Jesus' legal father. Remember the specific words, "no man of his seed shall prosper sitting on the throne." Jesus was not of Jeconiah's seed.

Okay, so that satisfies the two requirements, that Messiah be in the kingly line, but not *biologically* in the kingly line.

But that doesn't quite do it yet. There's one more requirement:

> ***2 Samuel 7:12*** *And when thy days be fulfilled, and thou shalt sleep with thy fathers, I will set up thy seed after thee, which shall proceed out of thy bowels, and I will establish his kingdom.*

> ***Psalms 89:3*** *I have made a covenant with my chosen, I have sworn unto David my servant.* ***:4*** *Thy seed will I establish for ever, and build up thy throne to all generations.*

> ***Psalms 132:11*** *The Lord hath sworn in truth unto David; he will not turn from it; Of the fruit of thy body will I sit upon thy throne.*

Adoption doesn't help here. Yes, Christ can be adopted into the kingly line to avoid the curse, but He cannot be adopted into the general family of David; He must be a biological descendant of David. So, how does that happen? Simple. Mary. Jesus was the son of God, but he was also the son of Mary, and Mary was a biological descendant of David.

How do we know that? For two reasons. First, because Paul said so.

> ***Romans 1:3*** *Concerning his son Jesus Christ our Lord, which was made of the seed of David according to the flesh.*

And that Davidic line could only be from Mary because Jesus had no earthly father.

But second, because the genealogy that Luke provides us is more likely to be a genealogy of Mary than of Joseph, unlike Matthew's genealogy, which can only be Joseph's.

> ***Matthew 1:6*** *And Jacob begat Joseph the husband of Mary, of whom was born Jesus, who is called Christ.*

> ***Luke 3:23*** *And Jesus … being (as was supposed) the son of Joseph, which was the son of Heli.*

The meaning of Matthew's "begat" is indisputable—Joseph's biological father is Jacob. But Luke's "son of" is very disputable, for three reasons anyway: *First,* Luke's Heli is certainly a different person than Matthew's Jacob. *Second,* the word "son" doesn't even occur in Luke's Greek text; we only infer it, and that inference could just as well be wrong. And *third,* "son of" has myriad meanings—e.g., Jesus is called son of Joseph, but he wasn't; it was "supposed," and son of God, and son of David, and son of Abraham.

Dr. Henry Morris[1] explains it this way: Joseph was clearly the son of Jacob (Matthew 1:16), so this verse (Luke 3:23) should be understood to mean "son-in-law" of Heli. Thus, the genealogy of Christ in Luke is actually the genealogy of Mary, while Matthew gives that of Joseph. Actually, the word "son" is not in the original, so it would be legitimate to supply either "son" or "son-in-law" in this context. That's enough. This discussion could go on and on, and you can find more information all over the internet.

---

[1] Morris, Henry. *The Defender's Sunday Bible.* Iowa-Falls, Iowa: World Publishing, Inc., 1995. Note for Luke 3:23.

So, back to the subject, and putting it all together, here are the three requirements to being Messiah:

1. Christ must legally be from the kingly line. Jesus was. He was Joseph's heir.
2. Christ must not be biologically from the kingly line. Jesus wasn't. He was adopted.
3. Christ must be a biological descendant of David. Jesus was. He was Mary's seed.

That's a lot of complicated requirements, and Jesus fulfills all of them, and He's the only one who does.

Now you might wonder, why would God go to all that trouble? The answer must be to eliminate all pretenders. No one could fake that pedigree. You either have it or you don't. There's no way to manufacture it.

What does it mean? It means that Jesus is the son of Mary, the son of David, the son of God, the king of the world, whose right it is to rule and who will rule, and our Savior. You probably should commit your life to him.

> ***1 Timothy 6:15*** *Which in his times he shall shew, who is the blessed and only Potentate, the King of kings, and Lord of lords;* ***:16*** *who only hath immortality…to whom be honour and power everlasting. Amen.*

Building on the Foundation Rock

Matthew 7:15, 26

At the conclusion of the Sermon on the Mount, Jesus talks about two kinds of false disciples: false teachers and false hearers.

> ***Matthew 7:15*** *Beware of false prophets which come to you in sheep's clothing but inwardly they are ravening wolves. Ye shall know them by their works.*

These are the false teachers. They have a lot to say, but they are lying. Their message is wrong. Their intent is wrong. Their words are wrong.

But besides false teachers, there are also false hearers.

> ***Matthew 7:26*** *Everyone that heareth these things of mine and doeth them not shall be like unto a foolish man which built his house upon the sand.*

These are false hearers who hear and pretend to listen to the true message but are not listening. Or they are hearing the false message. Either way, their hearts are wrong.

Teachers and students have one thing in common: their genuineness, or lack of it, is known by only one thing: continuing obedience to the Word. Whether they speak it or hear it, do they do it? That alone validates their salvation. Here's a short list that makes the point clear:

1 Corinthians 15:2 *By which also are ye saved if ye keep in memory what I preached unto you.*

John 8:31 *If ye continue in my word, then are ye my disciples in deed.*

Colossians 1:21 *...now hath he reconciled...if ye continue in the faith grounded and settled.*

1 John 2:3 *And hereby do we know that we know him, if we keep his commandments.*

Notice that these verses have two things in common: (1) present tense reality, and (2) future tense condition. Let's go through it again so you see the implication clearly.

1. *ARE saved...IF ye keep...*
2. *ARE my disciple...IF ye continue*
3. *NOW reconciled...IF ye continue*
4. *We know him* [now]*...IF we keep*

These verses are clear enough: by keeping his word in the future, we don't *become* His disciples, we *are* His disciples, *now*.

But how can that be? It's like cause and effect backwards, the effect before the cause, which is absurd. How can something in the future cause something to happen now? Can't. Then what are these words really saying?

There are two things these verses are not saying. (1) They are not saying you are a Christian without conditions. Clearly, there are conditions, namely, future obedience. And (2) they are not saying that your current Christianity is caused by your future obedience, which simply cannot be. What these verses are saying is that if you are a Christian now, that necessarily causes you to continue in obedience. That you continue is the proof that you are in Christ. That's the only way to make sense of it.

The perfect illustration of this is Jesus' picture of a man building a house either on rock or on sand. When the house is finished, the foundation is invisible, below the surface. But even so, out of sight, out of mind, the foundation is what it is, either firmly rooted in rock or precariously rooted in sand, and you can't tell just by looking at how the house is built. But the storm knows. The steadiness or the flimsiness of the house is revealed when, and only when, the storm hits, when the house on the rock will stand, and the house on the sand collapses.

Here's the point: that hidden foundation was built *before* the storm, not *during* the storm.

Too many Christians think that they are not yet rooted in Christ because the storm hasn't blown their way yet. That may or may not be. But either way, it's not the storm that makes them what they are, the storm only exposes what they are: rock Christians or sand Christians. Whichever they are, they are that *now.* If you're a rock Christian, you're fine. If you're a sand Christian, well, you might think about rebuilding.

Final note: Who is that rock?

Psalms 18:2 *The Lord is my rock and my fortress…*

1 Corinthians 10:4 *They drank of that spiritual Rock that followed them: and that Rock was Christ.*

In the hymn "The Solid Rock" by Baptist minister Edward Mote are found these words:

When all around my soul gives way,
He then is all my hope and stay.

On Christ the solid rock I stand,
All other ground is sinking sand.

Suffering for Jesus

1 Peter 2-4

Jesus suffered for us; should we be willing to suffer for Him? The Bible author who deals with this subject more directly than any other is Peter. The reason he deals with it so frankly is that he had no choice—persecution was coming, and it could not be ignored. That, and something else.

> ***1 Peter 1:1*** *Peter, an apostle of Jesus Christ, to the strangers scattered throughout Pontus, Galatia, Cappadocia, Asia, and Bithynia.*

Galatia? Asia? Why was Peter suddenly sending letters to Asia? That was Paul's territory. Peter's area was Israel and Egypt. Why was Peter encroaching on someone else's mission field? Here's the clue:

> ***2 Peter 3:15*** *And account that the longsuffering of our Lord is salvation: even as our beloved brother Paul also according to the wisdom given unto him hath written unto you.*

Why was Peter reminding Paul's churches what Paul had already told them?

The conclusion is not hard to reach: Paul was dead, executed by a headsman's ax by order of Nero. These good Christian people of Asia were feeling tremendous loss and were fearful. These letters from Peter to them were appropriate, and this was the right opportunity to discuss the frightful prospect of the coming Roman terror, and to discuss what God expected of them.

What did God expect of them during these coming trials that they could not avoid? Jesus and Paul had much to say about the price of discipleship:

Mark 13:13	*Ye shall be hated of all men for my name's sake.*
John 15:18	*The world hated me before it hated you.*
Romans 8:36	*For thy sake we are killed all day long.*
2 Corinthians 1:5	*The sufferings of Christ abound in us.*
Philippians 3:10	*The fellowship of his sufferings.*
Colossians 1:24	*afflictions of Christ in my flesh.*

The world doesn't hate us, in particular; it's Christ that the world hates. But once their hate had killed Him, He was no longer in their reach, so the world had to turn its gun sights elsewhere. Since there was a lot of hate left over, since it could no longer reach Him, where was it to go? Well, if Christ is in you (***John 17:23***), then guess what? You're the target.

You can either be quiet and get along just fine with the world, or you can do what God has asked you to do: ***2 Timothy 2:19*** *name the name of Christ.* This means be vocal about your Christianity. Name his name out loud. If you do that, some of the hatred that the world targets toward Jesus Christ will find its mark in you.

But is that fair? Look at it this way: Since Jesus suffered for our sins and took the sword meant for us into his own soul (***Luke 2:35***), is it too much for Him to ask us to take a few darts that are meant for Him?

Here is what Christ asks us to do:

> ***1 Peter 2:21*** *For even hereunto were ye called: because Christ also suffered for us, leaving us an example, that ye should follow his steps.*

So Christ set the example, and He expects us to follow. What exactly is His example? To suffer? To die? Maybe. But everyone dies at some point. So it's not simply suffering or dying that's the issue but *how* you suffer or die. Here are Peter's four rules of suffering and maybe dying:

[1] Be Innocent

1 Peter 2:22 *Who did no sin.* Whatever injustice you are called upon to endure, make sure that it is undeserved. Be completely innocent so that your suffering is unjust.

[2] Be At Peace

1 Peter 2:23 *Who when he was reviled, reviled not again.* Don't complain about it.

[3] Be Forgiving

1 Peter 2:23 *...he threatened not.* Don't threaten to get even.

[4] Be Trusting

1 Peter 2:23 *...but committed himself to him that judgeth righteously.* However you face death, trust God that your life, this one and the next, is in His hands.

[5] Conclusion

Ultimately, there are two ways to die: (1) for Christ, and (2) anything else. Since you have to die anyway, if you are one of the fortunate few who are allowed to die for Christ, that's a good thing. That is a glory that will follow you through the eternities.

> **1 Peter 4:13** *But rejoice, inasmuch as ye are partakers of Christ's sufferings; that, when his glory shall be revealed, ye may be glad also with exceeding joy.*

> **1 Peter 5:10** *But the God of all grace, who hath called us unto his eternal glory by Christ Jesus, after that ye have suffered a while, make you perfect, stablish, strengthen, settle you.*

If you are one of those called to make the ultimate sacrifice for Jesus, then later in heaven those sacrifices will be to you great glory. That's how Peter saw it, as did the thousands of brave Christians who followed Christ and Peter to their own crosses, lions, and burning stakes. Because of their sacrifices, their faith came down to us as something worth dying for. The importance of Christ's gospel is marked for all time by the blood of those willing saints who paid so high a price for Him and for us. May we be as worthy if God calls us to our own crosses.

The Three Temptations of Jesus

Matthew 4:2-11

No one escapes temptation. Not even Jesus. And the devil made Jesus a special target because everything depended on Jesus. If Satan could make Jesus fall, the war for the souls of men would be over.

There is a great deal for us to learn about Satan and his thinking from the three temptations that he poses to Christ.

[1] First Temptation: Doubting God

> ***Matthew 4:2*** *And when he had fasted forty days and forty nighst, he was afterwards an hungered.* ***:3*** *And when the tempter came to him, he said, If thou be the Son of God, command that these stones be made bread.* ***:4*** *But he answered and said, It is written, Man shall not live by bread alone, but by every word that proceedeth out of the mouth of God.*

So, what's the big deal about bread? Is bread a sin? If I go to the kitchen and make a slice of toast, am I sinning? No, of course not. But just about everything that people do can be a sin, or not, depending on the circumstances. If I bring that toast into a living room full of kids, and I give it to one kid while ignoring the others present, there is a high likelihood that a fight will erupt: "Hey, don't I get one?" Even my generosity, it seems, can at times be a sin. Intimacy in marriage is no sin; outside of marriage, it is sin. Killing a chicken is or is not a sin depending on who owns the chicken. Bread is not a sin but can be if it stands between you and God. A beach house, a Mercedes-Benz, an attractive person who stirs your chemistry, anything, including food, is not intrinsically sinful but has the potential (and only the potential) to stand between you and God, and become a sin. If you are morbidly obese so that those carbs you love are threatening your life, I'm sorry, but you've made food sinful. If you're in an important meeting where important decisions are being made, and you *have* to duck out for lunch even though everyone else is staying to work, and you return to learn that all the important decisions were made without consulting you, that's pretty much like sin. And your pitiful excuse, "but I was hungry," won't impress anyone. They were, too, but they stayed and took care of business. You didn't. Now they know that as far as you're concerned, food is more important. Yes, there are times and circumstances where innocent food can be sin. Satan is here manipulating food, very innocent food, to create a stumbling block for Jesus to trip over.

Jesus was in the desert to commune with God. Satan was there to prevent it, and he took advantage of Jesus's hunger. Forty days is a long fast, and Satan rubbed Jesus' nose in it: "My goodness, Jesus. God has left you stuck out here in the desert, no food, starving to death, and you, the Son of God. My, my. God is not taking good care of you, is he? Well, you'd better take care of yourself. Take charge. Here, change these stones to bread. Use your wonderful abilities to serve yourself. Go on, you have a right to it. God's will doesn't apply here because God has abandoned you. He's not living up to his part of the deal, so you'd better take care of yourself."

Another aspect of this temptation is Jesus' divine power. He had full creative power before He was born (***John 17:5***), then surrendered it at birth (***Philippians 2:6***). At His baptism, the Holy Spirit came and restored all of that to Him, bringing divine power to earth. That, in fact, is what precipitated Jesus going to the wilderness to *be* tempted. And now, Satan poses the logical question: To what end? How is He to use that power? For what purpose? To feed His own hunger or for something else?

Do you see the point of all this? The temptation is not Jesus's right to satisfy his hunger, but that his hunger was somehow incompatible with His being the son of God. In other words, if God is God, He would treat you better; therefore, you have a right to do what you want to do. That's the temptation. God has abandoned you, so take charge and grab what you can, which leads to the final wrong conclusion, which is so easy to fall into: "I can't believe in a God who would allow *that* (some evil thing) to happen."

Note too that God intentionally makes His point with something so trivial and innocent as bread. If the story had turned on a more glaring sin, such as adultery or murder, the point would be entirely lost. The sinful "thing" is not the issue here. The issue is anything at all—fill in the blank—that causes you to doubt God so that you set aside His interest to satisfy your own interest. That is sin. So God makes His point with innocent bread so that we won't fixate on the bread.

The broader spin is this: "If God is God, there wouldn't be evil in the world, children wouldn't be starving in Africa, my brother wouldn't have died in that car wreck," or whatever. Here, our reason to disbelieve and disobey is based on the idea that God has failed to live up to our expectation of what He ought to be, and therefore, He can't be God. God has abandoned me; therefore, I am justified to abandon Him and seek my own way.

Do you hear Satan whispering that in your ear? Do not believe it. It is a lie. God has never abandoned you. When people don't get what they want, they feel deprived, abandoned, as though God has forgotten them, and that is their excuse to take what they want, even if it violates God's will. "But I have a right to it." That's the justification.

And what was Jesus's answer? "I'm here for God's word, not bread."

So, how should you handle temptation in such times when you are really convinced that God has abandoned you? C.S. Lewis wrote it best at the end of Screwtape letter XIII. In it, the senior devil, Screwtape, writes this advice to a junior devil, Wormwood: "Our cause (stealing souls) is never more in danger than when a human, no longer desiring, but still intending, to do our Enemy's will (God's will) looks round upon a universe from which every trace of him seems to have vanished, and asks why he has been forsaken, and still obeys."

Amen to that. Have you ever felt completely abandoned? Have you ever really lost faith? Here's what you should do: obey anyway. And why not? Frankly, what have you got to lose? Your life? That's gone anyway. Remember this simple truth: It is not bread that keeps you alive; it is God who made the bread who keeps you alive.

[2] Second Temptation: Tempting God

> ***Matthew 4:5*** *Then the devil taketh him up into the holy city, and setteth him on a pinnacle of the temple.* ***:6*** *And saith unto him, If thou be the Son of God, cast thyself down: for it is written, He shall give his angels charge concerning thee: and in their hands they shall bear him up…* ***:7*** *Jesus saith unto him, It is written again, Thou shalt not tempt the Lord thy God.*

Exaggerating an opponent's point into absurdity is a sly and effective debate tool. That's the ploy that Satan now uses against Jesus. Satan first tried to get Jesus to not trust God. Satan failed because Jesus knew that life is sustained not by bread but by God's provision. That set up the second temptation, which is:

"Oh, so you trust God, do you? Well, if you really trust God, prove it. Go on. I dare you."

There is a difference between trusting God and tempting God. Trusting God is belief that has nothing to prove. Tempting God is unbelief demanding proof: "Betcha can't."

Now, unbelief is not automatically bad. We all start there. Unbelief that wants to believe can be a good thing, as in ***Mark 9:24*** *Lord, I believe. Help thou my unbelief.* But cynical unbelief, which rhetorically demands "betcha can't," God rejects that kind of unbelief. And then worse than unbelief is laziness pretending to be faith: "Why work? God will take care of me." And even worse still is indulgence: "We can't afford that car, but let's buy it anyway because God will take care of us." That's lust masquerading as faith. There are many ways to tempt God.

These two temptations of Christ show us two sides of the same coin. There are two principles here, polarized but equally true. The first principle is to trust God. The second principle is to obey God. The first *assures* us, as in ***Romans 3:23***, *being justified freely by his grace.* The second *commits* us, as in ***Philippians 2:12***, *Work out your salvation with fear and trembling.* Do these two principles contradict? If they don't exactly contradict, they at least tense up against each other like two tectonic plates pushing against each other in opposite directions, creating lots of friction and eventually earthquakes. Here we have two competing truths with lots of friction as they chafe against each other. And Satan works us from both sides. To Jesus he said, "If you won't do a miracle for yourself (make bread), then force God to do one for you (Jump!)" To us, Satan says, "If you have grace, then you are free to sin." How do you argue against such reasoning? Simple. God said, "Don't!" That's exactly Jesus' argument: "Don't!"

If Satan can't keep you from the truth, he will try to push you past it. Be very careful when you are trying to understand two competing truths, such as grace versus works. The temptation is to embrace one and reject the other. If there are two sides to the coin, remember that God gave you the coin. Jesus gave us the perfect example of this balancing act: Trust God, yes, but don't tempt Him.

[3] Third Temptation: Selfish Greed

> ***Matthew 4:8*** *The devil…sheweth him all the kingdoms of the world and the glory of them* ***:9*** *And saith unto him, All these things will I give thee, if thou wilt…worship me.*

Finally, Satan removes the mask and reveals his true intention: "What I really want is for you to worship me," and he offered the entire world.

In the first two temptations, there was at least a pretense, a reasoning that made those temptations seem justifiable. Here, there is none, and therefore it is the most dangerous of the three. Here, Satan is saying, "Forget right and wrong. Just do the bad thing, and I'll give you what you want." The first two temptations attempt to trick our conscience with reason. This temptation sidesteps reason altogether and entices us to abandon our conscience, not because we deserve something but just because we want it.

Why did Satan think this might entice Jesus? Jesus already owned the world. He created it. So just what was the temptation? The world belonged to Jesus, but Satan held it hostage. There is a legal adage: possession is $^{9}/_{10}$ of the law, which, while not literally true, illustrates that if you have something, the law assumes you own it until someone proves otherwise. And so we have a divine ownership dispute, a cosmic game of keep-away. Jesus is right to say, "Give it back, that's mine," but Satan insists, "Prove it. I have it, I'm keeping it, and I'll only give it back if you beg for it." But Jesus will not beg for it, will not worship Satan; instead, He will go to the cross and purchase it with His own blood, thus establishing, as we would say, a clear title so that Satan has to hand it over.

Satan knows something about us, that we will fight harder and compromise more to get back something that is rightfully ours to begin with. "Want it back? Worship me, and it's yours." That's the appeal, to get back what's rightfully Jesus's without the struggle, without the cross.

There are always two ways to get what we want. Satan's way, which is easy but wrong, and God's way, which is hard but right. Which did Jesus choose?

> ***Matthew 4:10*** *Then saith Jesus unto him, Get thee hence Satan: for it is written, Thou shalt worship the Lord thy God, and him only shalt thou serve.*

For Jesus, the right way led to the cross. Satan wasn't disputing ownership, he was just saying to Jesus, "Why go to the cross to win the world when I can give you the same thing without the pain?" Such a deal. There was just one problem: God forbade it. God will not permit us to worship anyone but God. The only way open to Jesus was the cross.

It is tempting to get what you want by easy means. Why work if you can steal? Why study if you can cheat? Why marry if immorality provides the same pleasures? Why tolerate people who get in your way if you can just kill them? Why do right, which is hard and sometimes painful, when doing wrong is easy and offers the same rewards? Why? Because it's what God wants from us, and because when you take what is not yours, guess what? It's still not yours. But what God gives you by your own diligent hard work and personal sacrifice is yours, for real and forever. Reject

Satan's easy, cheating ways to get what you want, and don't worry so much.

Philippians 4:19 *My God shall supply all your need.*

[4] Temptation In General

One extra point: Who deserves the most credit? The strong believer who obeys, or the weak believer who obeys? Hum. The strong believer has a greater motive, a high expectation of reward. But what of the weak believer who also lives right but has little expectation of reward? Does that obedience count for more? I don't know. Just something to think about.

Another extra point: God called Job "perfect."

Job 1:8 *And the LORD said unto Satan, Hath thou considered my servant Job, there i none like him in the earth, a perfect and an upright man, one that feareth God, and excheweth evil*

But Satan challenges that.

Job 1:9 *Doth Job fear God for nothing?*

And then he makes his case. Of course, Job is "perfect," Satan argues, but that's only because he has everything he wants. If a man truly has no desire for, say, wild women or booze, where is the so-called "righteousness" in being faithful or sober? *True* righteousness can only be measured by rejecting something you want but shouldn't have. In a word, sacrifice. Without sacrifice, God, how can you possibly know that Job or any other person is, as you say, perfect?

Satan's argument is sound. How do we know? Because God listened to him, as did Jesus in the temptations. Should we listen to Satan? My answer is: How can we not? His words are constantly ringing in our ears. Resisting temptation is not about blocking his voice, "La-la-la, I can't hear you," it's about hearing his argument, understanding his point, and rejecting his offer. And that necessarily begins with something you want.

God did understand Satan's point and *agreed* with him, and basically said, "You know, you're right. Well, let's remedy that. Give him something to want. Take everything from him, then we'll see how he behaves when he wants something that he doesn't have." And that's what the rest of the Book of Job is about: how he behaves when he is dispossessed.

Now, I'm not saying that one kind of righteousness is superior to the other. I am saying that either is equal to the other, and thank God for grace.

The story does have a semi-happy ending, and God's first opinion of Job is vindicated. It's a long story of temptation and trust and loyalty and other virtues and vices, but it all comes to a head at a single moment. After Job has endured all the philosophical arguments—temptations really—thrown at him by his friends, God has had enough. Not with Job—Job has persevered through it all wonderfully—but with his friends. God is angry with them and might even kill them. But they are rescued when Job prays for them. That's the pivotal moment. Even at the height of his own despair and problems, Job was more concerned for his friends' welfare than his own.

> ***Job 42:7*** *the* LORD *said to Eliphaz the Temanite, My wrath is kindled against thee, and against thy two friends: for ye have not spoken of me the thing that is right, as my servant Job hath.* ***:8*** *Therefore take unto you now seven bullocks and seven rams, and go to my servant Job,*

and offer up for yourselves a burnt offering; and my servant Job shall pray for you: for him I will accept: lest I deal with you after your folly. ***:10*** *And the* L*ORD* *turned the captivity of Job, when he prayed for his friends.*

Now, let's be a little careful here. Yes, God rewarded Job with lots of good things, but his first ten now dead children were not resurrected and restored to him. Yes, God gave him ten more children, and that's wonderful, but I'd still pine for the ten I'd lost. Wouldn't you? The real point is that we are required to accept from God the evil He sends our way as well as the good. Oh yes. It was evil that God sent to Job, there's no escaping that, and it couldn't be undone.

Job 42:11 *Then came there unto him all his brethren, and all his sisters, and all they that had been of his acquaintance before…and comforted him over all the evil that the* L*ORD* *had brought upon him…*

So the real point is not just that God rewards righteousness, but that God requires the righteous to accept from Him whatever He sends their way, good and evil. Credit God for the good and don't blame Him for the evil, but accept that He has a right to do that too, and maybe even has a purpose behind it. As far as reward goes, well, that's a matter of faith in the life after death that Jesus promises. And, finally, it is alright to feel overwhelmed by this great and confusing God.

Job 42:2 *I know that thou canst do everything, and that no thought can be withholden from thee* ***:3*** *Therefore have I uttered that I understood not; things too wonderful for me, which I knew not.* ***:6*** *Wherefore I abhor myself, and repent in dust and ashes.*

To feel inferior and humbled by the almighty God, and to have a God we can feel inferior and humbled by, really is a safe place. I also feel inferior and humbled by the sun, but it will one day go nova and eat us up, and that's not very comforting. But this creator God who actually lives and loves us enough to deliver us, now that's comforting. The good that He does for us is *so* good that it far overshadows the bad He allows. So, enjoy the good, walk away from the bad as best you can, and trust that God really is on our side—in the big scheme of things.

[5] The End

So, how does this story end, this conflict between Jesus and Satan?

> ***Matthew 4:11*** *Then the devil leaveth him, and behold, angels came and ministered unto him.*

Just do what's right. The devil will leave, and angels will take care of you. It doesn't mean that Satan is gone for good; he comes back (***Matthew 16:23, John 22:3***), but it does mean that Satan is gone for now.

The Gift Versus the Giver

John 6:26-50

The morning after Jesus fed the 5000, the same crowd showed up again—for breakfast. "Wow," they thought. "We found a guy who can make food. We want more of that." Entitlement was really on their minds, not salvation.

> ***John 6:26*** *Ye seek me not because ye saw the miracles, but because ye did eat of the loaves and were filled.* ***:27*** *Labour not for the meat which perisheth but for the meat which endureth unto everlasting life.*

In other words, Jesus was saying, "You're here for more free food, aren't you?"

The situation gave Jesus a perfect teaching opportunity. It set up a good metaphor to teach the people about himself and the allegiance he wanted from them. But they couldn't get their minds off the free food.

> ***John 6:28*** *What shall we do that we might work the works of God?*

What they wanted to know was how can we make food out of nothing? That was not the question Jesus wanted to hear from them.

> ***John 6:29*** *This is the work of God…believe on him whom he has sent.*

His point is clear: Get your mind off the gift and get your mind on the giver. Forget the food, that's just stuff that perishes anyway. Instead, focus on me. If I can give you food, I can give you eternal life. But they were undeterred. It was the food they wanted, so they argued.

> ***John 6:30*** *What sign shewest thou…that we may believe?* ***:31*** *Our fathers did eat manna in the desert.*

How peculiar. "If you want us to believe you, show us a miracle." But what had they just seen? If creating food out of nothing is not a miracle, then what is? The point is, they didn't want a convincing miracle because they didn't want to have to believe. They wanted free food! They wanted their entitlement.

But what about the miracle of the free food that they had already seen? Oh, that doesn't count. Why? Because that's an old trick. Moses fed our fathers manna. That's been done. Show us something new. This is not faith looking for confirmation, this is willful disbelief looking for justification. You fed us one night. Moses fed us for forty years. Top that! Actually, he did.

> ***John 6:35*** *I am the bread of life…* ***:49*** *Your fathers did eat manna in the wilderness and are dead.* ***:50*** *This is the bread* [me] *which cometh down from heaven, that a man may eat thereof and never die.*

What a stunning message. He did indeed upstage Moses. True, he had fed them one night, and Moses for forty years. But they were missing the point. The manna had lasted only forty years while the bread Jesus was offering, his eternal life, was forever.

But they couldn't get off the free bread, so they used his metaphor as a pretext.

> ***John 6:41*** *…they murmured…because he had said, I am the bread.*

Forget the sermon, where's the food? They were getting hostile.

Gifts are supposed to endear the recipient to the giver. They don't always. Sometimes we think that gifts are owed to us, and sometimes we love the gift but hate the giver. God gives us good things: life, health, money, church, family. Which of those things do you love more than God? God wants you to know that these are love gifts, unearned and unowed. But there is one gift that God has given that is better than all the rest, the one he really wants us to be most grateful for.

> ***Romans 3:24*** *Being justified freely by his grace through the redemption that is in Christ Jesus.*

Justification, redemption, eternal salvation, and all by grace, all for free. Now that's a love gift worth having. But we do need to love the giver more than the gift.

The Lie That Proves the Truth

Matthew 28:2-15

Who were the first witnesses of the resurrection? Peter? John? Mary? Actually, none of the above. The first witnesses were someone you wouldn't expect at all.

> ***Matthew 27:66*** [the priests] *went, and made the sepulcher sure, sealing the stone, and setting a watch.*

> ***Matthew 28:2*** *And, behold…the angel of the Lord descended from heaven and came and rolled back the stone from the door, and sat upon it.* ***:4*** *And for fear of him the keepers did shake, and became as dead men.* ***:11*** *…some of the watch came into the city, and shewed unto the chief priests all the things that were done.*

These were the first witnesses to the resurrection: Roman guards, eyewitnesses to supernatural events that nearly scared them to death.

Now, we don't know exactly what else they saw, but we know that they saw an angel rolling away the stone. How could they have known that unless they saw it? Whether they saw the risen Lord or not is unclear, but they saw enough to know the tomb needed to be investigated. And so they did, and they found it empty.

Unfortunately, though, they lied about it. Still, you can learn a lot from a lie.

Matthew 28:12 [the priests] *gave large money to the soldiers.* ***:13*** *Saying, Say ye, His disciples came by night, and stole him away while we slept.* ***:14*** *If this come to the governor's ears, we will persuade him, and secure you.* ***:15*** *So they took the money, and did as they were taught: and this saying is commonly reported among the Jews until this day.*

What do we learn from this lie? First, it proves absolutely that the tomb was empty. Second, it proves that there is no natural explanation for the tomb being empty, because the guards had no better story than the one they made up, and that story is impossible to believe. And why is their story impossible to believe? Because: **[1]** If the guards had fallen asleep during their watch, they would have been executed. That's why they were uncomfortable with the lie because it incriminated them, so they needed assurance (and a great deal of money) from the priests to protect them from the governor. **[2]** We cannot imagine disciples rolling away the large, sealed stone without waking the guards. Indeed, when the angel rolled away the stone, it *did* wake the guards. **[3]** We cannot imagine disciples who fled when Jesus was alive suddenly getting brave now that he is dead. All but John and Peter had run from Gethsemane and remained in hiding for days. **[4]** How could the guards know what happened while they were asleep?

So the account given by the priests and the guards is not only a lie but a conspicuous lie.

And where does that leave us? With an empty tomb and no natural explanation as to how it got empty.

But there is a perfectly good supernatural explanation, which is what the angel said:

Matthew 28:6 *He is not here: for he is risen.*

The Parable of the Unjust Steward

Luke 16:1-14

The parable of the Unjust Steward is the strangest thing Jesus ever said, that we know about. Why? Because it is difficult to believe that He actually meant what He said, that a crook deserves praise.

Let's review it quickly; then I'll take a shot at making sense of it. You may like my interpretation, or you may not. Whatever. Mine is just another opinion of this tricky text.

> ***Luke 16:1*** *And he said also unto his disciples, There was a certain rich man, which had a steward; and the same was accused unto him that he had wasted his goods.* ***:2*** *And he called him, and said unto him, How is it that I hear this of thee? Give an account of thy stewardship; for thou mayest be no longer steward.* ***:3*** *Then the steward said within himself, What shall I do? For my lord taketh away from me the stewardship: I cannot dig: to beg I am ashamed.* ***:4*** *I am resolved what to do…*

So the steward, because of incompetence, dishonesty, or laziness, has mishandled his boss's affairs and is now about to lose his job. He has a short time left to get things in order (clean out his desk) and wonders how he can use that time remaining to his advantage. He hatches a plan, makes a decision, and goes for it. Let's continue.

> ***Luke 16:4*** *I am resolved what to do, that, when I am put out of the stewardship, they may receive me into their houses.* ***:5*** *So he called every one of his lord's debtors unto him, and said unto the first, How much owest thou unto my lord?* ***:6*** *And he said, An hundred measures of oil,*

And he said unto him, Take thy bill, and sit down quickly, and write fifty. ***:7*** *Then said he to another, And how much owest thou? And he said, An hundred measures of wheat. And he said unto him, Take thy bill, and write four-score.*

So the steward's plan was simple. While he was "cleaning out his desk," he was still his boss's agent with full signing authority. And that enabled him to execute a devious plan: He would receive discounted payments from creditors and credit the accounts as paid in full. This would ingratiate him with those creditors who he expected would reciprocate later in some way. In short, he was a crook embezzling from his boss to the advantage of creditors and himself. All of that is simple, but now the baffling part.

Luke 16:8 *And the lord commended the unjust steward, because he had done wisely; for the children of this world are in their generation wiser than the children of light.*

It is a stretch by any means that a boss, ripped off by his thieving employee, would then say, "At-a-boy. You did a great job stealing from me."

I have read several explanations of how this could be so, and none of those explanations ring true, not to me anyway.

I have my own explanation, which (like any other) may or may not be true. My explanation was that Jesus was being sarcastic. We should allow Jesus to use all the speech devices that we ourselves use. Indeed, throughout the gospels, we do see him using humor, metaphors, exaggeration, anger, even name-calling (pigs, dogs, vipers, whited sepulchers)—why should we deny him literary license to be sarcastic? I think he rolled his eyes and conveyed with other body language (which Luke fails to mention) that he didn't really mean it. I think a more accurate translation would be something like: "And his boss told him, 'You did a great job.' Because after all, bankers are smarter than prophets. Right? Yea, right!" In other words, it's nonsense. You *don't* get rewarded for stealing. That's the point in my reading.

But now, what about the next verse where Jesus seems to add his own approval to the boss's?

> ***Luke 16:9*** *And I say unto you, Make to yourselves friends of the mammon of unrighteousness; that, when ye fail, they may receive you into everlasting habitations.* ***:10*** *He that is faithful in that which is least is faithful also in much: and he that is unjust in the least is unjust also in much.* ***:11*** *If therefore ye have not been faithful in the unrighteous mammon, who will commit to your trust the true riches?* ***:12*** *And if ye have not been faithful in that which is another man's, who shall give you that which is your own?*

I think Jesus is now conceding something to his own fictional characters. He is saying in essence, "I'll give them this: You do need to stay friends with the world. Go to school, get a job, work, produce, so that you can survive. If you're not good at handling money, how can you handle the things of God? The Unjust Steward is *not* going to get complimented or re-hired or promoted; he's going to get fired. He can't handle his boss's money, what makes you think he can handle his own?"

:12 convinces me that I'm correct to believe that ***:8*** is sarcastic. It is exactly the opposite conclusion. ***:8*** says the boss compliments the Unjust Steward. ***:12*** says, no way. Either ***:8*** is sarcastic, or ***:8*** and ***:12*** contradict each other. I prefer to believe that ***:8*** is sarcastic.

Now let's finish this off.

Luke 16:13 *No servant can serve two masters: for either he will hate the one, and love the other; or else he will hold to the one, and despise the other. Ye cannot serve God and mammon.*

Jesus turns this whole story of the Unjust Steward on its ear. While he concedes that we have to get along in the world by taking care of business, he quickly pulls us away from that "balanced" view and reminds us that we can't have it both ways. As much as you'd like to, you can't be dedicated to both money and God. You must decide which will dominate your life. Which moves you: money or God? This was exactly the problem the Pharisees had.

Luke 16:14 *And the Pharisees also, who were covetous, heard all these things: and they derided him.*

As I said, my interpretation may not be correct, but I think it is correct, and it at least makes sense. Some other explanations I've read don't even make sense.

Villains, Heroes, and Christ

Romans 5:6-8

What is the difference between villains and heroes? Villains cause injury to help themselves, and heroes endure injury to help others.

Most people are not villains or heroes. Most are just ordinary people disinclined to do or suffer injury—they just want to get along and not get involved. Villains and heroes find themselves on the fringe of society quite apart from more ordinary people.

As heroes go, some are more heroic than others. In particular, some of the most heroic would *lay down his life for his friend* (***John 15:13***). They are the "cut above" heroes—the most heroic heroes, those who would die for another.

But there is one hero in *that* group (the most heroic heroes) who stands above them all and is the most heroic of the most heroic heroes. And that hero is Jesus Christ.

What sets Jesus apart from all other heroes is not his willingness to die (many heroes do that), but for whom he was willing to die.

Think of heroic examples: A mother jumps in front of a rushing car to save her child. A fireman runs into a burning building to save a trapped person. A soldier faces gunfire to save his nation. Some will risk their lives, but always for those who are, in some sense, deserving.

But what about undeserving people? Who dies for them? Not me. There are people I would risk my life to save, and there are people I know I would not risk my life to save. But I'm not Jesus. Now this question: Who did Jesus die to save?

> **Romans 5:6** *For when we yet were without strength, in due time Christ died for the ungodly.* **:7** *For scarcely for a righteous man will one die: yet peradventure for a good man some would even dare to die.* **:8** *But God commendeth his love toward us, in that, while we were yet sinners, Christ died for us.*

Let's make sure we understand what Paul is saying. Are there heroes who are brave enough to die for someone else? Yes, there are, but only for "a righteous man" would a hero dare to die. The point is that not even heroes will die for an unrighteous man—except, that is, Christ, who did, in fact, die for us *while we were sinners.*

Let's say this another way. What most people would not do for us, even if we were worthy (although if we were worthy, some heroes would dare), Christ did for us when we were unworthy.

Let's say it still another way. If we were good, then God would not need all that much love to save us. Everyone wants to save the lovable, the cute, the pretty, the smart, the good. We all seek good things. That's our nature. But if we are ungodly sinners who have all come up short? Then the love that seeks to save such people must be a very great love indeed.

Who did Christ die for? Ungodly sinners. Some are heroes, some are villains, and some are just ordinary folk. But Christ's heroic love offers salvation to all.

Is it not interesting that this doctrine was written by Paul, who was, by his own admission, the world's greatest sinner? And why did God have Paul in particular pen this? Because: ***1 Timothy 1:16*** *…for this cause I obtained mercy…for a pattern to them which should hereafter believe.* In other words, if Jesus could save Paul, he could save pretty much anybody.

Abide in the Vine

John 15:1-11

Jesus used many metaphors to characterize himself. Here is one:

> ***John 15:1*** *I am the true vine…*

A vine is a living thing. Since Jesus says elsewhere, ***John 11:25*** *… I am…the life,* that he depicts himself as a living vine makes sense. And if we are branches growing from that vine— ***:4*** *the branch cannot bear fruit of itself, except it abide in the vine*—that makes sense too.

Here are four blessings that accrue to those who remain "in the vine."

[1] You Will Bring Forth Fruit

> ***John 15:5*** *I am the vine, ye are the branches: He that abideth in me, and I in him, the same bringeth forth much fruit: for without me ye can do nothing.*

Vines, productive vines, produce fruit: grapes, berries, whatever. It's a pleasure to walk by and pick and enjoy a handful of free berries that nature so willingly provides. Jesus says He is like that, and we can be that too, if we are plugged in. There is no such thing as a fruit-less saint.

Why is your fruit important? Because God wants you to have a productive life. Not just to have lived and died, but to have mattered to someone else. Every Christian matters to someone.

Galatians 5:22 *But the fruit of the spirit is love, joy, peace, longsuffering, gentleness, goodness, faith,* ***:23*** *Meekness, temperance, against such there is no law.*

Colossians 1:10 *…be fruitful in every good work.*

John 4:36 *And he that reapeth receiveth wages and gathereth fruit unto life eternal life…*

[2] Your Prayers Will Be Answered

John 15:7 *If you abide in me, and my words abide in you, ye shall ask what ye will, and it shall be done unto you.*

God never promised to answer the prayers of unbelievers. He may or may not; that's His choice. But He has promised to answer the prayers of believers, those in Christ, in the vine.

Psalms 37:4 *Delight thyself in the Lord and he shall give thee the desires of thine heart.*

[3] Your Fruit Will Glorify God

John 15:8 *Herein is my Father glorified, that ye bear much fruit*

It's one thing for God to glorify us, but for us to glorify God, that's a privilege. Any child who loves his parents seeks to glorify them. "Mom, Dad. See what I did? Are you proud of me? Did I make you happy?" God is like any proud papa who delights in seeing his children do well.

[4] YOUR JOY WILL BE COMPLETE AND FOREVER

> ***John 15:11*** *These things have I spoken unto you that my joy might remain in you, and that your joy might be full.*

God is not a cosmic party-poop. It is not His self-appointed task to make you miserable. I hope it does not come as a surprise to you, but God actually wants you to be happy. But He knows something that apparently most people don't know: that people can only be happy if they live by God's standards.

The joy that God offers, unlike the joy the world offers, is (1) complete [full], and (2) permanent [remain].

Living Water

Matthew 5:6

A favorite analogy that Jesus used for his parables was water. Why He would choose that image is no mystery since we cannot live long without it.

[1] The Need

> ***Matthew 5:6*** *Blessed are they which do hunger and thirst after righteousness for they shall be filled.*

Humans cannot live long without water—in the desert, three days, tops. And when a human is deprived of water for any length of time, the resulting thirst will become agonizing to the point of total fixation. A man dying of thirst wants nothing else except water. A delicious prime rib steak will not do. If, on the other hand, he's dying of hunger and not of thirst, the steak is what he desperately craves. Whatever he is deprived of, that is what he desperately seeks. That's the image Jesus creates for us in this beatitude.

Humans have a desperate need for righteousness, and God is anxious to fill that need, but only for those who desperately want it. How do you know if you thirst for righteousness? If you do, then nothing else will satisfy that craving: not money or any of the things that people long for. Guilt, like thirst, causes a person to fixate on one thing: relief.

Luke 16:24 *have mercy…send Lazarus that he may dip the tip of his finger in water and cool my tongue.*

In the parable of Lazarus and the Rich Man (if it is a parable), the rich man finally got thirsty, but too late. He finally craved water or righteousness when none was available.

[2] The Source

So, if we need righteousness like a thirsty man needs water, where can we look to find it? Certainly not ourselves. If a thirsty man could just look in his pocket and find water, he wouldn't be thirsty in the first place. Instead, he has to look to some other source.

Philippians 3:9 *Not having my own righteousness, but God's.*

If we have no righteousness of our own to satisfy our thirsty souls, what righteousness is available? God's righteousness. And where is that?

John 4:13 *Whosoever drinketh of the water that I shall give him shall never thirst; but the water that I shall give him shall be in him a well of water springing up unto everlasting life.*

A vivid picture. Not just water, but a well of water that never runs dry. And with the continual flow of water unabated comes continual life, eternal life. The significance of this particular parable is that Jesus is speaking it to a woman who is living with a man to whom she is not married. He is offering her eternal life if she drinks the water of righteousness that He is willing to give.

That's the best kind of water there is: eternally, thirst-quenching righteousness.

John 8:36 *If any man thirst, let him come unto me, and drink.*

People who aren't thirsty don't drink. I don't drink when I'm not thirsty, and that's a problem because my doctor tells me I should drink more water. But how can I do that when I'm not thirsty? Righteousness is available, but only to those who are thirsty for it, enough to come to the well and drink.

[3] THE PRICE

Water costs. Yes, I know, you just turn on the faucet and water flows out freely. Well, it isn't free. The city and its taxpayers spend billions of dollars to make that water flow freely to you every time you turn on that tap.

So, what about the righteousness that Jesus offers so freely? Did it cost Him anything to offer it? Actually, it cost him a lot.

John 19:38 *I thirst.*

Psalms 69:21 *…in my thirst they gave me vinegar to drink.*

This was no parable. It was for Him a horrible reality and a fulfilled prophecy. On the cross, Jesus was deprived of everything. All the things that he offered so freely to us, He had to pay for. Here's a list:

John 19:28 *Jesus knowing that all things were now accomplished, that the scripture might be fulfilled, saith, I thirst.*
He became thirsty so you could drink.

2 Corinthians 8:9 *…though he was rich, yet for your sakes he became poor, that ye through his poverty might be rich.*
He became poor so you could be rich.

Romans 6:10-11 *For in that he died, he died unto sin once: but in that he liveth, he liveth unto God.*
He became dead so you could live.

2 Corinthians 5:21 *For he hath made him to be sin for us, who knew no sin; that we might be made the righteousness of God in him.*
He became sin so you could be righteous.

John's Witnesses

The Gospel of John

John's purpose in writing his gospel was to tell us who Jesus is and to present the evidence. Some of that evidence is the testimony of eyewitnesses, those who saw and heard important things and freely told us their experiences. Their words ought not to be ignored, and we should pay attention.

Here then is John's list of witnesses. It's impressive:

[1] JOHN THE BAPTIST

> ***John 1:6*** *There was a man sent from God, whose name was John.* ***:7*** *The same came for a witness, to bear witness of the Light, that all men through him might believe.* ***:29*** *The next day John seeth Jesus coming unto him, and saith, Behold the lamb of God, which taketh away the sin of the world.*

There were many Old Testament prophets who said that the Messiah was coming. But John was the first to say He is here, right here, right now. And he probably pointed and said, "He's standing right there. See him?"

[2] A PHARISEE

> ***John 3:1*** *There was a man of the Pharisees, named Nicodemus, a ruler of the Jews.* ***:2*** *The same came to Jesus by night, and said unto him, Rabbi, we know that thou art a teacher come from God: for no man can do these miracles that thou doest, except God be with him.*

Nicodemus understood what so many failed to understand, then and now: the miracles were the proof that Jesus was who He claimed to be.

Please don't make too much of the "by night." Some think he was sneaking around, trying to visit Jesus when no one would see him. He wasn't sneaking around, he just came to Jesus in the evening when he got off work, the same as you would do.

[3] A Gentile Woman

> ***John 4:29*** *Come, see a man, which told me all things which ever I did. Is not this the Christ?*

Jesus had just told her that she was living in sin. ***:18*** *…he whom thou now hast is not thy husband…* People get annoyed when their sins are pointed out to them. Not this woman. She was just excited to have found the Messiah, and she wasted no time proclaiming Him to her friends.

When Jesus points out our sin to us, what is our reaction? Annoyance? Hatred? Or gratitude that forgiveness is available?

[4] The Miracles

> ***John 5:36*** *But I have greater witness than that of John: for the works which the Father hath given me to finish, the same works that I do, bear witness of me, that the Father hath sent me.*

Anybody can say anything. "Words, words, words," said Eliza Doolitle to Freddie in *My Fair Lady*. Then she demanded, "Show me!" Well, Jesus did. Over and over. His miracles were His witness. ***10:38…*** *though ye believe not me believe the works.*

[5] God

John 5:37 *And the Father himself, which hath sent me, hath borne witness of me. Ye have neither heard his voice at any time, nor seen his shape.*

God bore witness of His son in several ways: prophecy, miracles, His own verbal declaration at the baptism, and by His spirit. All of these, the people somehow missed.

Note that "ye have neither heard his voice" cannot be general. People had indeed heard God's voice—people at the baptism and at the Mount of Transfiguration had heard His voice. Jesus is simply saying to these particular people, God has borne witness of me; too bad you missed it.

[6] The Scriptures

John 5:39 *Search the scriptures, for in them ye think ye have eternal life: and they are they which testify of me.*

So you think you've found eternal life in the scriptures? Well, it's good that you're reading them, but you need to read them again. I'm there, and you've missed me. Yes, you find eternal life in the scriptures, but only if they lead you to find me.

[7] Jesus Himself and His Father

John 8:18 *I am one that bear witness of myself and the Father that sent me beareth witness of me.*

Of course, Jesus bore witness of Himself. Anyone with a message must put themselves on the stand, so to speak, and claim his message as his own. "Don't shoot the messenger" was not a defense for Jesus. He was the messenger, but He was also the message.

But He was not alone. How many witnesses did the law require? ***Deuteronomy 17:6*** *...two witnesses, or three witnesses...* Why? Because one witness can lie. Two can be examined separately to see if their testimonies agree. Jesus claimed He was the Christ. Anyone could say that of themselves, but in Jesus' case, God confirmed it. God was a second witness.

[8] The Comforter

John 15:26 *But when the comforter is come, whom I will send unto you from the Father, even the Spirit of truth, which proceedeth from the father, he shall testify of me:*

Beyond words, beyond deeds, the Holy Ghost is a miracle that happens in the hearts of every believer. We believe because we cannot not believe. God put it in us to believe.

[9] The Disciples

John 15:27 *And ye also shall bear witness, because ye have been with me from the beginning.*

That includes you. Once you came to the truth, Jesus called you to proclaim it so that others can benefit from your witness.

[10] Summary

Why all these witnesses? Well, because:

John 20:31 *But these are written, that ye might believe that Jesus is the Christ, the Son of God; and that believing ye might have life through his name.*

The claim before us, which we are required to decide—that Jesus is the Christ—is so important that God wants to make available to us the best possible evidence. So that, at the very least, if we decide wrongly, it won't be because of a shortage of reliable witnesses.

Thank you for reading

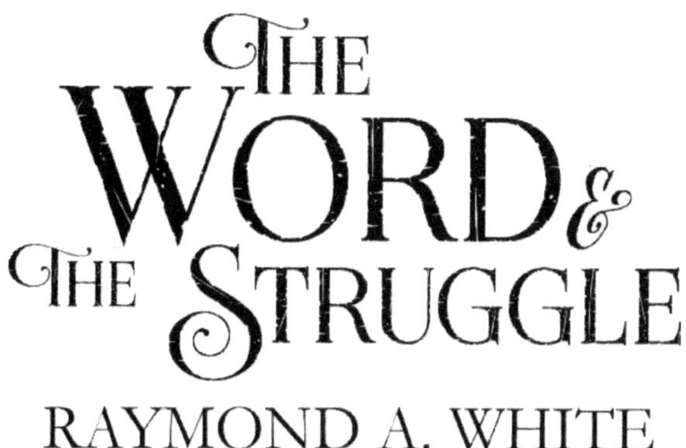

VOLUME IV: JESUS CHRIST

Please post a review on your favorite online retailer.

To receive updates about the release of the next book in this series,

VOLUME V: MARRIAGE & PARENTHOOD

please join Skyrocket Press's email list here:
www.skyrocketpress.com

About the Author

Raymond A. White is a retired computer programmer who spent the bulk of his career at Jet Propulsion Laboratory working in the field of deep space exploration. He is also a lifelong student of scripture, having dedicated more than forty years of his life to studying ancient history and the Bible. In addition, Mr. White is the father of three adult children and the grandfather of fifteen grandkids and four great-grandchildren. He lives in Southern California with his daughter and her family.

Learn more at:
http://www.skyrocketpress.com/

Read an excerpt from

The Word & the Struggle

Volume III: The Character of Man

Anger

Proverbs

Proverbs 12:16 *A fool's wrath is presently known: but a prudent man covereth shame.*

When a fool loses his temper, he is proud of it, maybe he even brags about it. When a wise man loses his temper, he is ashamed of it and wants to conceal it. There is this saying: "A wise man is twice angry, the second time with himself." If you must get angry, at least have the sense to understand how foolish you were and apologize to everyone who was unfortunate to overhear your tirade. A fool doesn't get it.

Proverbs 14:17 *He that is soon angry dealeth foolishly…*

It is not anger per se that God hates, even Jesus got angry, and certainly God gets angry. But it's the quick anger, the short fuse temper, that's generally a bad thing.

Proverbs 14:29 *He that is slow to wrath is of great understanding: but he that is hasty of spirit exalteth folly.*

Again, wrath is justified at times, but it must be slow wrath, thought out to some degree. Before you engage, ask yourself these questions: Is this fight worth picking? Is this the hill you want to die on? It may be, but be sure first.

Proverbs 15:1 *A soft answer turneth away wrath: but grievous words stir up anger.*

The way to start a fight is to say angry words. You can usually avoid a fight with careful words. When angry words are spoken to you, the knee-jerk reaction is to respond in kind, be a mirror, answer anger with anger. But that turns an initial hostility into a full-blown fight. But if you instead answer that initial hostility with calm words (okay, you talk, I'll listen), inquiring words (so I'll understand, what exactly are you angry about?), maybe even confessing words (yes, I used your pliers and forgot to put them back, sorry), usually that will calm the other person down and restore peace.

It's all in the tone. Anything you have to say can be better said in a soft tone. Even things that are deadly serious and laced with rage, like "I want a divorce," can be said civilly. Whatever the issue, however negative, it can be better dealt with without the shouting.

Proverbs 15:17 *Better is a dinner of herbs where love is, than a stalled ox and hatred therewith.*

I love a rich man's prime rib (stalled ox) more than a poor man's diet of broccoli. But if the broccoli is served in a home of love while the beef in a home of anger, I'll take the broccoli.

Proverbs 15:18 *A wrathful man stirreth up strife: but he that is slow to anger appeaseth strife.*

Sometimes, to avoid a fight, you need to just slow down a bit. Just don't act from reflex. Pause. The delay of even a few seconds can often give you control of your temper.

Proverbs 16:32 *He that is slow to anger is better than the mighty; and he that ruleth his spirit than he that taketh a city.*

Anger is not just about families; sometimes it is political. Nations go to war because someone is angry with someone else. If you must go to war, of course, you must win. But isn't it better to avoid the conflict by staying calm and seeing if everyone can be made happy with a compromise?

Proverbs 19:19 *A man of great wrath shall suffer punishment; for if thou deliver him, yet thou must do it again.*

Uncontrolled anger must be met with a negative response of some kind. If it is not, then the anger will be repeated again and again. Uncontrolled anger should not be treated with impunity, otherwise the angry person will become an incorrigible sociopath.

Proverbs 25:28 *He that hath no rule over his own spirit is like a city that is broken down, and without walls.*

This is a man with an uncontrolled temper. But not just a temper, "no rule over his own spirit" refers to any kind of compulsive behavior that he indulges without restraint. Anger is one such behavior to be sure. Promiscuous sexual indulgence is another. Drug addiction, gambling, too much television, too much food, too much sleep, too much whatever — all such uncontrolled behaviors are destructive and are like a city *without walls*; in other words, he has no defense, he is vulnerable to the inevitable consequences.

Proverbs 26:21 *As coals are to burning coals, and wood to fire; so is a contentious man to kindle strife.*

Generally, a fight begins because someone just likes to argue, or, as my dad used to say, someone has a "contrary nature." Or we might say that such a person just has a bad attitude or is always trying to assert control, trying to get others to submit.

Proverbs 29:22 *An angry man stirreth up strife…*

What would be amusing, if it weren't so maddening, is how surprised angry people are when their unrestrained anger causes others to be angry with them. What do they expect to happen? Surrender? Anger causes anger. How do you get that simple idea into the head of perpetual troublemakers? It must eventually dawn on them that *they* are the cause of the incoming anger, and *they* could have prevented it by not being angry in the first place. The anger directed at them is just a reflection of their own anger.

Proverbs 30:33 *Surely the churning of milk bringeth forth butter, and the wringing of the nose bringeth forth blood: so the forcing of wrath bringeth forth strife.*

You think that your verbal shot will be the last word, but it won't be. Instead of being the last word, your angry shot will only escalate the battle. You need to understand that the other person will respond to every verbal abuse, and there will be no *last word.*

Ecclesiastes 3:8 *…a time to hate…*

It's tempting to think that there's never a right time to hate. This verse says otherwise. When is it right to hate? I'm sure that if I had discovered the Auschwitz concentration camp in 1945, I would have hated the Nazis as much as any other Allied soldiers. And I do not feel inclined to forgive Muslim suicide bombers who specialize in blowing up children. I'm just pointing out that there are times when hatred is appropriate.

How about Jesus? Did he ever hate anyone? If not quite hate, he was certainly angry with false religionists who used their privileged position to enrich themselves at everyone else's expense and called that "service to God." That's why Jesus cleansed the temple. And if you think he regretted doing it, then why did he do it twice?

> ***Ecclesiastes 7:9*** *Be not hasty in thy spirit to be angry: for anger resteth in the bosom of fools.*

The advice is not don't ever get angry, but don't get angry quickly or easily. When a person is quick to get angry, it's because anger *resteth in the bosom*, anger is in his or her heart, and such people are fools. A peaceful person, who does not bear anger in the heart, might still get angry, but if so, the anger has been thought out and is justified.

www.ingramcontent.com/pod-product-compliance
Lightning Source LLC
LaVergne TN
LVHW020043110826
845155LV00029B/617

* 9 7 8 1 9 4 7 3 9 4 1 6 2 *